The Glasgow Gigs

K. A. ARNSIDE

Grosvenor House
Publishing Limited

This book is published by
Grosvenor House Publishing Ltd
Link House
140 The Broadway, Tolworth, Surrey, KT6 7HT.
www.grosvenorhousepublishing.co.uk

A CIP record for this book
is available from the British Library

Paperback ISBN 978-1-83975-944-4
Hardback ISBN 978-1-83975-945-1
eBook ISBN 978-1-80381-078-2

*In memory of Arnold Z. Arnside, the world's
greatest unpublished storyteller...
... and...
... to those who believe that buying an album is
better value for money than going to a gig...
... financially, you are correct. But...*

CONTENTS

GOING TO A GO-GO

The online ticket scrum didn't always exist. There was no internet in the 80s, so there was no virtual gun being held to your head with the ultimatum that you have four minutes and 20 seconds to complete your purchase. Even the internet's predecessor, the 'speed dial, redial, curse and try again' ritual had no place in society. In the 80s ticket purchasing was far more gladiatorial than that, and facing a disgruntled cashier who just wants to say 'next' enough times to get to the end of their shift was a truly intimidating experience. And there was always the chance that you would be the one who queued for hours only to reach the ticket window in time for it to be slammed in your face. Nobody wanted to be THAT PERSON.

Some things, though, never change and bands jacking up interest in their upcoming offerings prevailed as much then as it does now. It's just that the marketing platforms were different.

Not that anyone from the 80s would have talked about marketing platforms. In fact, all talk of platforms had been left behind in the 70s. Music press, radio shows, posters, word of mouth. That was good enough to get the word out and there was one band in particular who only had to snap the fingers on their 10 collective hands and the world would come running.

***

So, I'm sitting at work one Thursday morning in May and The Shugmeister calls. This was not entirely unusual. But the urgency in his voice was. He needed answers – now – no time to lose. He had heard it on Radio Clyde. If I wanted in, I had to say yes, there and then, otherwise…

He had pleaded with his boss for some time off, at short notice, like today, like now. The boss's last name was Furrie. Pronounced Fury. The phonetic pronunciation was more reflective of his personality. He knew there was no point in resisting.

I had said yes. Of course I had. Opportunities like this only came round once in a lifetime. All previously arranged engagements could be rescheduled. I hung up the phone and waited… and trusted… and hoped.

***

The operation was precision personified, although the strategic details were unknown to me at the time. There was a dual purpose. Tickets for *The Concert* and tickets for Scotland v England. Two acquisitions of gold dust in the same morning? Surely it wasn't possible?

The Shugmeister couldn't drive, but he knew someone who could, someone who had a vested interest in all of this, too. It wasn't difficult to get in touch with that someone, as he was sitting opposite. It made negotiations with The Furrie more difficult. Not one, but two of them wanted to be excused. It was a two-man job. It was the only way it would work. The Furrie was having none of it but promises of 'making up the time' and 'you won't regret it, boss' won him round and the mission was on.

They knew the queue would already be forming so time was of the essence. The Driver would take The Shugmeister right up to the door. The Driver would then depart the scene and pick up the briefs for Hampden. That was a done deal, but they could only get two so I was out. The Driver would then return to The Apollo and circle the building, as many times as it took, until The Shugmeister emerged victorious with the treasure.

They hadn't banked on the queue being quite as long as it was. The power of Radio Clyde and the worshipping musical faithful had come together as one. From the door of The Apollo the queue went down Renfield Street, round the corner and into Sauchiehall Street. If you started at the door of The Apollo and tried to find the end of the queue it would have been a very disheartening experience indeed.

In fact, even after you found your place in the queue and crawled at a snail's pace to the door, you had to factor in the real sting in the tale. The door wasn't the end of the journey. Once you made it inside, the sight that greeted you made your heart sink further than the depth of the ocean. The queue stretched on, through the foyer and on, up the stairs, and on, and on, and on and who knew where it would end. And who knew if today was the day that you would be THAT PERSON.

This was the dilemma that greeted The Shugmeister as he took up his place. All he could do was wait. All he could do was hope. There was no point in checking his watch. The queue would move whenever the queue moved. The prize was more important that the detail. Promises had been made. Four tickets required. One for him, one for The Driver, one for me and one for the other guy. Let's just call him A.N. Other, like they used to in the *Green Citizen* or the *Pink Times* when they didn't know the names of all the players in the teams of lower league clubs.

The queue snaked on and The Driver continued to circle. Gradually, Sauchiehall Street became Renfield Street. Time was going on. It was getting close to lunchtime. Burger King had been resisted, as had Lauders Bar. The Furrie would only tolerate so much. The next landmark was Renfrew Lane. Once The Shugmeister got past that he was near the door. Once he was in, he would see the queue continuing, but he knew about that part. He looked upstairs. He pictured the sight. He knew the tickets would be disappearing. He didn't want to be THAT PERSON.

He was on the stairs now. Near the top. He could see the ticket windows, tantalisingly close. Someone moved away, tickets in hand. The next person moved up. That person wasn't going to be THAT PERSON. They moved away, gleeful look on face, tickets in hand. And the queue moved on. Only a few in front now. Please don't let him be THAT PERSON. And the queue moved on. He couldn't be THAT PERSON. And the queue moved on and it was his turn next and the person in front moved away and the window didn't close and that's when he knew. He was not going to be THAT PERSON.

***

'Four tickets for The Stones please', he said, sweat on his brow, cash in his hand.

'They're limited to two per person.'

Time stood still. He struggled to gather his thoughts. His life flashed before him. Why had he made those promises? He was the one who made the sacrifice. Him and The Driver. They were the ones who were in debt to The Furrie. But how was he going to explain it? Two people were expecting him to appear with tickets to see The Greatest Rock 'n' Roll

4

Band in the World. He did the only thing that any self-respecting person could do in the situation. He pleaded, but anyone who has ever pleaded with a bored ticket seller on the other side of a window in The Apollo will know that this only ever had a limited chance of success.

'It's very clear. Two tickets per person. Do you have anyone else with you?'

'No, but…'

'Well. You can only have two tickets then. There are hardly any left… and people are waiting.'

'I know but… you don't understand… can you talk to your boss?'

'There's no point. Two tickets per person. Do you want two tickets or not?'

That was it. There was no way out. He would just have to explain it to me and A.N. Other. He was sure we would understand. He had tried everything. He knew we would be disappointed but it would be OK, wouldn't it? But the feeling in the pit of his stomach was bad. He ran his fingers through his hair, put his head in his hands and turned away in disgust. Maybe he thought this show of displeasure would make the ticket seller change her mind. Maybe she would make an exception, just for him.

But the agitated sight he saw behind him made him realise he had to act fast. The natives were getting restless. The woman behind was struggling with a little boy, a toddler for whom the novelty of being there had worn off long ago. The faces of those behind said one thing and one thing only. If there are no tickets left by the time I get to that window your life won't be worth living. There was only one thing he could say.

'Excuse me, would it be alright if I borrowed your son?'

***

5

Genius! The mother consented. Of course she did. It provided welcome respite for her, the prospect of a little entertainment for the boy and some much-needed progress for the queue.

The toddler was presented on the counter at the ticket window.

'Four tickets for The Stones please.'

The ticket seller protested.

'I've told you. Two tickets per person. That's the rules.'

'Two for me and two for him.'

'Oh, come on. You're trying it on. I've told you the rules.'

'Could you check with your boss?'

She turned and looked for support. She motioned towards The Shugmeister but her boss had seen everything. He shrugged his shoulders. Two tickets per person. That was the rule and there were two people at the window. So, The Shugmeister left The Apollo with four tickets, the toddler left The Apollo with a pocket full of coins and The Driver screeched up to the door after his 48th revolution and they headed back to face The Furrie who turned out not to be too furious after he had been told the story of just what an ingenious worker he had.

***

When the phone call came through to confirm, I was elated. The Stones had been announcing gigs on local radio at one week's notice, stoking up a frenzy among their fans. That meant we only had a week to wait, so the arrangements were made. Next Thursday, The Ivanhoe, in The Buchanan Hotel, just beside the entrance to the subway, and then on to The Apollo to see The Greatest Rock 'n' Roll Band in the World.

CYMBALS AND SYLLABLES

What was the first record I ever bought? I can't give you a straight answer. Not because I can't remember but because I didn't buy just one. I bought two. I had a pound to burn and you could get two 7in singles for a pound in 1971.

The Shugmeister tried to influence me. If there was new music coming into the house, he wanted to tilt things in his direction. Being nine, I had my own ideas.

Eventually a compromise was reached and *My Sweet Lord* by George Harrison was purchased along with *The Pushbike Song* by The Mixtures. Later that same year, The Shugmeister's influence prevailed again. I wasn't feeling well and my dad was going into town. He said he would buy me a record to make me feel better. Apparently, I chose *You've Got a Friend* by James Taylor. I wasn't so sure at the time but was grateful to have it later.

***

What was the first gig I ever went to? I *can* give you a straight answer to that one. Slade, Glasgow Apollo, May 1973. Clearly my taste in music had become more sophisticated!

Considering I was only 11 I assume that a responsible adult was involved but I have no memory of this. I think I was with my school pal Stewpot, but can't be sure about that either. We had the same birthday, Stewpot and me. Still do. Big Hendy, too. Three boys in the same class with the same birthday. What are the chances of that? And Robert Burns for good measure. But he wasn't in my class at primary having been dead since 1796.

Anyway, I can't remember the peripheral details because the peripheral details were not important. Only the music was important. I had worn out the stylus at home playing *Get Down and Get With It* from 'Slade Alive' so I knew what it sounded like live on vinyl, and I wanted to hear it live on stage. By that time Slade had conquered the charts with number ones being totted up regularly, and my main concern was that *Get Down and Get With It* wouldn't make it onto the set list. I needn't have worried.

There was the usual tedium of the support act to deal with. Not easy to tolerate when you are 11 and all you want is to *Get Down and Get With It*. Not easy to tolerate when you are viewing the show from a great height and some gruff vocalist with a voice too deep to be audible is drunkenly groaning into a microphone that seems to be too close to his mouth. On top of that, the music barely gets going and, all in all, it is just too much of an inconvenience when you are 11 and your parents have paid for you to come and see a proper band.

Intervals are funny things. When you are 11 they just represent even more of a delay in seeing who you came to see. But it does mean you can go to the toilet and see if there are any sweets to buy. It also meant that The Sensational Alex Harvey Band were finished.

***

There isn't any need to describe Slade's show in detail. Noddy wore a comedy tie. Dave Hill had a stupid haircut. Jimmy Lea played his violin and Don Powell crashed muscularly on his cymbals and drums. The hits were churned out, one after the other. People got up and danced. People *Got Down and Got With It*. The audience shouted for more. Slade gave them more. The lights went on. Everybody went home. And nothing was ever the same again.

***

Sometimes, tickets just dropped into your lap. You didn't always have to queue from Sauchiehall Street, turn into Renfield Street, go through the foyer and up the stairs. Sometimes, someone would phone up and offer you a ticket. That's what happened to me and we shall call that someone Carduzzin.

Carduzzin probably doesn't know this, but he played a large part in teaching me what you can do with music. You can listen to it, obviously, but you can feel it, use it, play with it, get lost in it. It can make you dance; it can make you laugh; it can make you cry. It can make you sit on the floor at your best friend's engagement party, in a puddle of beer, pretending that you are rowing a boat just because the DJ played The Gap Band. But anyway...

When tickets drop into your lap you have a decision to make. It is unlikely to be tickets for a Beatles reunion. More likely to be for a band that the original purchaser is prepared to forego because a better offer has come their way. Either way, you have a decision to make. Take it or leave it. Cockney Rebel?

'Mmm... not sure... there is that one song... oh, and that one too... eh... OK... let's go for it.'

I expect that's what Carduzzin heard when he asked me to go along with him.

Almost two years had passed since that first Slade gig and I had been back to see them the following year. Slade were clearly a band that I wanted to see. Cockney Rebel? The truth is that, for me, their songs on the radio were great. Cockney Rebel on stage? Playing tracks from their album? Playing new music that nobody had heard yet? That was going to take some getting used to. I suppose my doubts would be answered, one way or another, once we got inside The Apollo, but that's when the confusion started.

***

The queue round the corner and into Sauchiehall Street wasn't just for when tickets were on sale. It applied equally on nights when bands were playing so we joined the queue and dug in for a long wait, on a cold night in February 1975.

Finding things to do in a long queue can be a challenge. Conversation is the obvious starter, but this tends to tail off after a while. Landmarks become important. A shop doorway, a street corner, the lane, the chippy. Tiny, incremental movements towards your destination. The gaps between these landmarks are tortuous. You try listening in to other people's conversations.

'Have you seen them before?'

'Do you have any of their albums?'

'Have you heard their new single?'

In other words, the same conversation I had just had with Carduzzin.

Then, it's time to look at the tickets. There is something comforting about a concert ticket. This is the confirmation that you have permission to enter. Permission to see the act in question. If your companion has been in possession of the tickets, there is something reassuring about just feeling the paper between your fingers. Cheap, tissue-like, raffle ticket quality it may be, but it brings with it a wave of serenity and excitement in equal measure. Never before has the name of a promoter seemed so intriguing.

'M.A.M. in association with TRIGRAM presents…'

Who cared what it meant? For me, it meant I would get into The Apollo. I would get in from the cold. I would get to see live music and I would get to see it tonight, Tuesday, 10 February 1975.

I looked at the ticket for ages. Something wasn't right. It was Tuesday, I knew that because the charts had been announced at lunchtime. But it wasn't 10 February. It was 11 February. I always wrote the date at the top of the page when copying down the chart. All I had been told was that the gig was on Tuesday. Carduzzin never said the date. Was 'Tuesday' a mistake? Had the gig already taken place, on Monday the 10th? But why were all these people here, standing in the queue? I did some quick calculations in my head, like you do when you are trying to work out what day your next birthday will fall on. I worked out that 10 February would fall on a Tuesday in 1976. Were we a whole year early? I dismissed the thought. Why would all these people be here, standing in the queue? But then I could hear those people having the same conversation that was going on in my head. Some of them were in doubt too. The queue started to move and we got closer to the door but I still wasn't sure if we were going to be turned away – 24 hours late or a whole year early.

I was overthinking it. We call them typos now. They can be resolved in a key stroke and confusion can be cleared up in any number of messaging formats. We didn't have a proper word for typos in 1975. Spelling mistake, gaff, balls-up, cock-up. They all meant the same thing, but they weren't official words, like 'typo'.

Cockney Rebel for their part, no doubt oblivious to the confusion in the queue, delivered a perfectly acceptable set. We knew enough about them to know that any music we hadn't heard before would be interspersed with a *Judy Teen* or a *Mr Soft*. There was theatricality about Steve Harley, who by this time had tagged his name in front of the band. He was, for the most part, Cockney Rebel and Cockney Rebel was, for the most part, Steve Harley. We didn't have much notice of this gig and, at the time we heard about tickets being available, we had no idea what was to come. THAT SONG entered the charts THAT WEEK. We must have been among the first people to hear it played live and it still makes me smile today, just as it did on the non-existent Tuesday, 10 February 1975.

***

It takes a bit of a leap to get from Slade and Cockney Rebel to Lionel Ritchie. Despite the middle-of-the-road-radio-twoness that the name conjures up, Lionel Ritchie was a funk-a-teer at heart. The Commodores came to The Apollo in 1979 in the midst of a vintage spell for those who liked to groove. The Jacksons, The Average White Band, George Duke, Van Morrison and Bootsy's Rubber Band had all been. Chic and Sister Sledge were still to come. Mix that with an assortment of Kinks, Stranglers, Stiff Little Fingers, Paul McCartney and Wings, Status Quo, Blondie, Roxy Music, Elvis Costello and Motorhead, and there was something for everyone. And, in case there is any doubt, 1979 gave us Chris De Burgh, Cliff Richard and Showaddywaddy too!

Standing in a very long queue to get into The Apollo didn't seem quite so bad on a Thursday night in August. Ticket in hand, girl by my side, decent seats in the stalls and an encyclopaedic knowledge of The Commodores recent output all helped. 'Machine Gun', 'Natural High', 'Commodores Live' and an album simply called 'Commodores'. They all had similar characteristics. Lots of brass, lots of bass, dripping with funk and at least one killer ballad.

Live albums can be hit or miss. Not 'Commodores Live'. All it did was make you want to be there, and now we were. The live version of *Zoom*, despite its ballad-like qualities, demonstrated a real ability to work a crowd. The word 'Zoom' may have been highjacked by video conferencing and any mention of it accompanied by Fat Larry's Band but, for me, 'Zoom' can only mean one thing – The Commodores.

Contrast that with the term 'brick house' which was intended to be complementary when directed at females, but I have a fair idea what would have happened to me if I had referred to any of the girls I knew as a brick house. However, the language of funk followed different rules and, even if they take the words away, the drum intro will still get me every time and the groove will live on.

The Emotions were the support act and they got things off and running and built up the required frenzy. *Best of My Love* was fresh in everyone's mind and, of course, they had to give us *Boogie Wonderland*. That song is synonymous with Earth Wind and Fire but, although they got the main credit, it was 'with The Emotions'. Maybe the girls were delighted to get their name on the record but for me it's a duet. A duet involving a huge number of performers, but a duet just the same. It wouldn't have been the same without them.

So, here's how a normal gig works. The support act say goodbye, the main act come on, say 'Hello Glasgow', sing some songs, whoop up the crowd, plug their album, sing some more songs, tell you you've been the best crowd ever, say goodnight, do an encore, say goodnight again, go to the hotel and wake up another city.

Well, that's how a normal gig works, but not The Commodores. The lights went out and we tingled with anticipation. There might have been some movement on stage but it was hard to tell. A noise came in from the distance, as if there was a train coming. A cymbal started tapping, prompting a cheer. A chorus of falsetto-like voices sang something, the letter C. The Apollo was still in darkness as they sang the O. Still darkness as we heard the M, and another M. Everyone had caught on and everyone was up on their feet. The mystery voices spelled out the rest and The Apollo was alight in a blinding flash. There, on the stage, right in front of us, the sight we had come to see. They had blindsided us. We were all playing catch up but The Commodores were playing *Machine Gun* and people danced and people cheered and no one had any intention of sitting down.

***

But sit down you must… at some stage. For all the *Machine Guns*, *Brick Houses* and *Too Hot Ta Trots*, there has to be an *Easy*, a *Zoom*, a *Three Times a Lady*. The Commodores wouldn't have been allowed out of The Apollo without singing them but Lionel Ritchie had piled a unique level of pressure on himself. He must have had some idea what it felt like to be Freddie Mercury trying to follow up *Bohemian Rhapsody*. *Three Times a Lady* had been a huge hit in 1978. Number one in the charts here, there and everywhere and the soundtrack to weddings, anniversaries and general fumblings at the end of many an evening.

Lionel took a bit of time out to quieten the audience. He sat at his piano and explained the process. He acknowledged that he had to come up with another *Three Times a Lady* and humbly offered his best shot. He told us the song was called *Still*. He sat at the piano and sang it within the hush that had descended on The Apollo. The song was greeted with a rapturous response and the full ensemble, equipped with sparkly catsuits, glitter and shades, kicked back into life and the party was on again. They left us with *Midnight Magic*. It wasn't quite midnight... and you can finish the rest of that sentence yourself!

***

Early 1974

Noddy: *I loike The Apollo but we can't ploy the're this year.*

Dave: *Whoi not, Noddy?*

Noddy: *'ere's a leest of places I wanna play.*

Dave: *This is never guin ter werk. Wolver'ampton, Chipping Norton, Cirencester, Shepton Mallet? Sum of them am OK. But I can't see Mönchengladbach worken.*

Noddy: *Whoi not, Dave?*

Dave: *Cos it's a UK tour, Noddy. And another thing, why yav yaouw picked Shepton Mallet, 'as it even got a theatre?*

Noddy: *'aven't got a clue, but it's got the roight number of syllables. We need places with four syllables.*

***

That is the conversation I like to imagine Slade having when planning their UK tour in 1974. We have already established that they played The Apollo in 1973 but one cataclysmic song had been released since then. The song that makes Noddy rub his hands on 1 December each year. I don't know if Noddy has kids, I don't know if they went to college but, if they did, this is the song that would have put them through. There was no way Slade couldn't sing it on the tour, it's just that the tour was taking place in the summer.

A decision was taken to replace the words 'Merry Christmas' with the name of the place in which they were playing. Glasgow didn't fit. But I'm sure Slade liked playing The Glasgow Apollo so common sense prevailed. Noddy provided an explanation on the night. He knew it was a Christmas song and he knew it was May. He knew we wanted him to sing it but it just wouldn't sound right. He gave us a few lessons, so that we knew our part, and did a few choruses, replacing 'Merry Christmas' with 'good old Glasgow.'

I don't know if Slade ever did play Chipping Norton... Shepton Mallet... or Mönchengladbach.

EUPHORIA...
SADNESS... AND
EMERGENCY RESCHEDULING

I might have been 20 years old, but my parents did what parents always do. They shared my excitement. I couldn't wait to tell someone, and they were first in line. It was like the day you come home from school with a painting that looks like a splodge, but you insist it is a cat and your parents tell you how wonderful it is. That's just what parents do and mine were no different.

I suppose they must have sensed my enthusiasm, maybe they had felt it themselves someday. Tony Bennett at The Glasgow Empire or some such thing. Neither of them would have thanked you for tickets to see The Rolling Stones but they had their own heroes and those heroes helped them relate to mine.

I don't know how long I ranted on for. The story about the tickets was hot off the press and they listened patiently. Arrangements were already in place, even though the gig was a week away, and they nodded and smiled politely. I speculated about what songs The Stones would sing and they kept their counsel as I spouted forth about *Miss You, Sympathy for the Devil* and *You Can't Always Get What You Want*.

There must have been a break in proceedings and they must have been relieved. Relieved to get back to the mundane routine of evening life. Cooking smells from the kitchen, TV programmes that ran from 7.20pm until 8.10pm, the sound of a fixed landline ringing and people stating their full number to whoever was calling. My parents must have been relieved. Relieved to get a word in. Relieved, because they needed to get a word in.

'Eh… bit of bad news today, I'm afraid. Big John died.'

I was poleaxed. I had known that Big John had been taken into hospital. I had been so caught up in my own excitement that I hadn't even thought to ask. I never thought it would come to this and couldn't think of a single thing to say.

'He passed away last night. We found out this morning. The funeral is next Friday.'

In my confused, selfish mind, I managed to calculate that the funeral wouldn't get in the way of The Stones gig. I admonished myself. What a thing to think and anyway, no one has a funeral on a Thursday night.

***

Big John and Auntie Isa were formative characters in my life. We lived directly upstairs from them. Two boys in our house, three girls in theirs. Our long, narrow hallway made the perfect arena for indoor football. The letterbox gave a rough approximation of a crossbar. Whoever was guarding the front door had to do a lot of diving, and falling, to protect their goal. The noise must have been unbearable.

'Oh, Isa, I don't know how you put up with it', my mother would say.

'Put up with what? We never hear a thing.'

That was just the way she was. Even when we started playing golf in the hall she wasn't fazed. And don't go thinking that golf is a quiet, sedate game. It can be, but not this version. You see, there was an old, wooden shafted iron and a batch of plastic, practice golf balls. We didn't use real golf balls indoors. We weren't savages. But there had to be a target. We needed something to hit the balls into and what could be more obvious than a bin... a *metal* bin.

'Clang!' The noise was particularly satisfying if the ball went in. First it bounced, then rolled around and around before coming to a stop, but even a near miss would send a sound through the house like a dinner gong.

'Oh, Isa, I don't know how you put up with it.'

'Put up with what? We never hear a thing.'

Even the commentary didn't provoke a reaction. Admittedly, my Peter Alliss was quieter than my David Coleman, but the sound must have carried, and Auntie Isa never said a thing.

***

Big John had taken me to my first football match... at Celtic Park. My dad's working hours didn't allow for football on a Saturday afternoon and Big John must have felt he had a duty to indoctrinate me into the ways of the west of Scotland. Having three girls of his own, he didn't get much of a chance to do that kind of thing. I was seven, the same number of goals that were scored in a routine trouncing by the dominant Old Firm giant against the plucky provincial pretender. I lost interest after a while and spent my time wandering around the terraces, collecting ring pulls from discarded beer cans. It was one of the most exciting days of my life.

Now, it occurred to me that 13 years had passed since that day. Big John's family had freed themselves of the anti-social noises from above and moved closer to the city. We had gone in the opposite direction, into Boundary Charge territory, but we still kept in touch. The world was a little poorer without Big John. This was the man who took his family on holiday from the East End of Glasgow to Stewarton. They went in a taxi! He bolted swings to door frames so that his children could have the joy of play, even if they didn't have a garden. This was a man who was willing to make an ill-advised leap from his veranda onto that of a downstairs neighbour because they had gone out and left a pot on. Big John's passing needed to be marked and I would have to be on my best behaviour at The Stones gig to make sure I gave him the respect he deserved.

***

Friday came and went. Six days to go before The Stones gig. Saturday was cup final day. A dominant provincial pretender dished out a routine spanking to a plucky Old Firm giant, after extra-time. There was extra-time at Wembley, too, and the FA Cup Final ended in a draw. That was the news every Scottish football fan wanted to hear as it meant we would get to see the replay live in an era when live football on TV was something of a rarity. I checked the scheduling to see when the replay would be. Thursday! This was almost as rare as a live game. Football only happened on Saturdays and Wednesdays. This was going to present something of a dilemma. How do you manage to watch the FA Cup Final replay and see The Rolling Stones at The Apollo when both events are happening on the same night? Plans had to be drawn up. What time was kick-off? What time was *The Concert* due to start? Did bands ever start on time? Was there a support act? Were they any good? Would it be worth going home from work and back into town? Should we head straight to The Ivanhoe? What if the replay went to extra-time?

***

The ticket for The Apollo provided no clues. All it said was that *The Concert* started at 7.30pm. This, of course, was intentional. If your marketing strategy is to take fans by surprise and create a ticket-buying frenzy, the last thing you want is someone at the printers blabbing about it. But bands never started on time. *The Daily Record* was forever championing the rights of girls from Aberdeen who had travelled to Glasgow to see The Bay City Rollers, only to find that they didn't come on stage until after 9pm and, by the time Les had sung *Shang-a-lang,* no matter how fast they ran with the gang the last train had long gone. We needed to know if there was going to be a support act and only The Bouncer could help.

I had gone to school with The Bouncer. He was a good guy on the whole, great goalkeeper, exuding the confidence that allowed him to sprint across the gym at dancing practice to ensure he wasn't left with a 'tottie', as Mr McCracken the PE teacher used to say. Different times.

The Bouncer supplemented his normal income with work in the evenings at The Apollo. If anyone could find out what we needed to know, he could. My problem was that I didn't exude the confidence to sprint across the gym and hadn't yet recovered from the sight of The Bouncer straddled across an armchair at a party five years before kissing the girl of my dreams. I wasn't prepared to make that call just yet.

We were going to have to wing it. Meet at The Ivanhoe at 7pm. That would give The Driver, AKA Lonesome Dave, enough time to have his esoteric debate about The Clash versus Marvin Gaye. The FA Cup Final replay would kick-off at 7.30pm. We were feeling confident about seeing the first half. Maybe even part of the second. We wouldn't be all that far from The Apollo – close enough that someone could nip round to check on proceedings. With a bit of luck we would see the bulk of the game and maybe, by that time, a clear winner would emerge. It was going to be tight but no one ever achieved great things by being sensible.

THE CLASH VERSUS
MARVIN GAYE

Lonesome Dave, for those of you who don't know, is the leader of The Blues Cowboys. They didn't achieve a lot of commercial success. It was always about the enthusiasm. They don't crop up in many musical anthologies and it is time someone put that right.

Lonesome Dave's taste in music is wide, varied and eclectic. His appetite is insatiable. He has travelled far and wide, from one side of the planet to the other, and music is always his mission. He lurches from one genre to another, never able to fully exhaust his need to hear something new. This does not make him dissatisfied; on the contrary, it feeds his passion.

Nova Scotian fiddles, Appalachian clogs, Caribbean steel drums, classical Steinways, African Mouth Music, human beat boxes, gospel choirs. Just your average line-up on *Later with Jools Holland*.

***

The Clash had already established themselves. Lonesome Dave was never a punk; maybe Joe Strummer wasn't one either. It didn't matter, Dave just loved the music. He loved the raw, irreverent, politically induced diatribe that flowed from the bands that had something to say. He laughed, along with the rest of us, at Jilted John and the others who climbed on board the bandwagon. But it was the bands with a cause that grabbed his attention.

When The Clash played The Apollo in 1981 there was a buzz. They had been before and others had seen them, but I hadn't. Their catalogue was well established but this was no greatest-hits band. There were causes that had to be highlighted. Almost every song was intellectually conceived and politically charged, and the music was more sophisticated than maybe they were given credit for. We were taken through funk, reggae and good old rock 'n' roll, stopping off at all points in between. They had to pay the bills, though, and the occasional *Should I Stay or Should I Go* or *I Fought the Law* didn't go wrong.

The aura of The Clash had not been lost on me but, like many other musical experiences, I was quite slow on the uptake. (I wasn't too sure about *Bohemian Rhapsody* when I first heard it.) Those around me saw things differently and slowly chipped away until I jumped on board and, by the time the gig came round, there was no band more important than The Clash.

You wouldn't have described it as a flash gig, but they really showed their credentials. This was no thrash, bash, shout, swear and spit gig. This was the real thing. People did jump up and down wildly, but people danced as well. It was a wall of noise with a tidal wave of social conscience crashing against it, flooding a very willing public.

There were those, who shall remain nameless, who made a pain of themselves by constantly drawling 'give us *White Man*'. I doubt the band could hear but they got it out of the way relatively early. Then they were able to get on with the rest of the show.

***

The contrast didn't really hit me until I thought back to earlier in 1981. Sometimes you just got tickets…

There was another gig that I didn't intend going to and only went because opportunity knocked – my friend Liz must have been behind it because I went along with her.

I wouldn't have queued to buy tickets for Ultravox but, when the offer was made, there were two main reasons for saying yes. The first was obvious – THAT SONG. You know, the one that was held off the number one spot by THAT OTHER BLOODY SONG. THAT SONG was a song that had to be heard live. The others I could take or leave. The second reason was that it gave me a chance to put right a wrong that I had suffered a few years before.

Everybody knows that Midge Ure was the frontman in Ultravox and everybody knows he was also the lead singer of Slik. Not many people know about the gig Slik played in Garthamlock Secondary School.

Slik might not thank me for saying this but they were one of the boy bands of their time. Perhaps not as big as The Osmonds or The Bay City Rollers but they had a couple of hits and adorned the walls of young girls' bedrooms up and down the country. If you paid any attention to the charts you couldn't fail to notice Slik. They had a number one with *Forever and Ever* in 1975 (more than THAT Ultravox song achieved, I hear you think).

Scottish country dancing was a big part of the curriculum at Garthamlock Secondary School in the 70s. The annual dance consisted of The Gay Gordons, The Canadian Barn Dance, The Dashing White Sergeant and all the rest. It didn't matter which year you were in, you had to learn them all. People from the 70s will know this already, even if they didn't go to Garthamlock, as they will have been press-ganged into learning these dances in their schools, too.

It also didn't matter if you preferred a different form of entertainment. The excitement of having a night when you could let yourself go was always tempered by the need for structured adherence to the rules and the faint cry of Mr McCracken:

'One, two, three
'Two, two, three
'Three, two, three
'Four.'

But one day, someone who knew someone, who knew someone, who knew someone, who knew Midge Ure had the brilliant idea of giving the senior pupils something they might actually enjoy – Glasgow's home grown, heart-throb chart-toppers – Slik.

My problem was that I wasn't a senior pupil. For those of us in the earlier years this option was off limits. It didn't seem right. I thought about some of the people who would get to go to this gig. People who didn't know a thing about music. Geeky people, prefects, Neil Sedaka fans! And here was me – someone who took an interest, someone who cared, someone who knew a thing or two about music – locked out, barred, excluded.

Not to be outdone I made my way up to the school on the night. I knew that entry would be impossible. Apollo bouncers had nothing on the bunch of teachers who kept order every day in our rough Glasgow comprehensive. I sneaked around, trying to find a vantage point out of sight. I just needed to feel like I was part of it. The noise, at best, was muffled. There were screams from inside, happy screams. I convinced myself that I knew which songs were being sung but I had no idea, really. It was like The Who at Celtic Park all over again. I was on the 5th hole at Lethamhill Golf Course that day. Depending on the direction of the wind, the peacefulness of a Saturday evening would give way to some indecipherable, amplified wave of sound. On the night that Slik played Garthamlock it was just the same.

***

Once we were in The Apollo with Ultravox, the visual spectacle was quite something. A lot was expected of The New Romantics. If you decided to make use of cutting-edge technology in your music you had to reflect this in all aspects of your being. Make-up had to be worn, hair had to have something to say, clothing had to be flamboyant, lyrics had to have meaning. Stage sets had to be up to speed, too. Light shows, lasers, special effects. Sound and vision, choreographed to perfection.

Midge Ure stood there, on stage at The Glasgow Apollo, long, moody overcoat unbuttoned, probably taking a moment to reflect on how far he had come since that night in Garthamlock. Dry ice swept across the stage. A drum sound emerged from the silence. Not a sound made by a real drum, but a drum sound just the same. One beat, then three. One beat, then three. One beat, then three, and the audience reacted. It was THAT SONG.

We got what we came for and plenty more on top. Smooth, professional, efficient. Some might say Slik. It would just have been nice if the drummer hadn't been sitting with his arms folded as drum sounds ricocheted off the walls of The Apollo.

***

And now, here I was, a few rows from the front, bang slap in the middle, salivating with anticipation for the entrance of The Clash but with increased expectations after the flamboyant staging at the Ultravox gig. I could see the stage clearer than I had ever seen it before. I knew how magical this arena could be. What surprises did they have in store? Answer? None!

The band bounded onto the stage, picked up their instruments, someone switched on a bunch of 100w lightbulbs and we were up and running. The following 90 minutes or so passed in a blur. I didn't know all the songs. I didn't know what all of them were about. I didn't need to.

***

Back in The Ivanhoe for some post-gig analysis I couldn't disguise my enthusiasm. What had I been thinking of worshipping Slade at the age of 11? What place did Steve Harley have in the world of true music? How could The Commodores waste their time rehearsing harmonies and dance moves so precisely? The bus to the future had arrived and I had finally jumped on board and was on a collision course with the establishment.

Lonesome Dave seemed to have different ideas and was extoling the virtues of Marvin Gaye. I couldn't believe it. Marvin hadn't had a hit for ages. Fair's fair, *Got To Give It Up* was a belter but it was years ago – 1977 – just around the time The Clash were coming to the fore. And it was just a disco song. Just something to dance to.

Lonesome Dave wouldn't be moved.

I took him to task.

'Surely there is more to life than someone churning out pop songs for people to dance to.'

He held his ground. I pressed my case.

'He plays Caesar's Palace these days and releases back catalogue tracks with Diana Ross and Stevie Wonder. He's good. Don't get me wrong… some of his songs are great… but does he have anything to say?'

Lonesome Dave referred me to *What's Going On* and *Trouble Man*.

I felt the moral high ground slipping a bit but persevered.

'With The Clash you can let off steam. You can have an opinion. You can jump up and down. You feel as if you're part of something. You feel like you can change the world. What can you actually do to Marvin Gaye's music?'

'Make love.'

There was no answer to that.

FEAR OF GOD IN
THE ARCHES

So far, you could be forgiven for thinking that there were only two music venues in Glasgow in the 70s and 80s – The Apollo and the dinner hall at Garthamlock Secondary School. This, of course, was not the case and gigs were performed in any number of places. One day, Lonesome Dave will tell his tales of meeting Muddy Waters at The Maryland, but that was one of many chance encounters that passed me by.

Smaller venues are, by their very nature, more intimate. The audience gets up close and personal with the acts. I shook the hand of Carey Bell on the Renfrew Ferry, Billy Connolly once borrowed my pen and John Hegley's puppet sniffed my genitals in The Mitchell Theatre. It doesn't get more intimate than that, and I speak as someone who was once whipped upstairs by a young lady in The Glasgow Royal Concert Hall.

There are great sections of the world that seem to have been closed off to me. Vibrant, creative ideas and spaces which human beings dream up and use and constantly take me by surprise. One such venue materialised one Sunday in, of all places, Scotstoun.

Around the time of Ultravox we also had Spandau Ballet, Duran Duran, Visage and Japan. They were bands who had found a new way to make music, who could make music in their bedrooms and carry their instruments under their arms and who shot to fame and spawned tens of thousands of pretenders to the crown.

The New Romantics didn't suffer the ordeal of boarding a bus with a double bass, knowing that they couldn't sit down and that, no matter how hard they tried, they would always be in everyone else's way. The New Romantics didn't have to deal with The Bam on the Bus either.

'Wow, that's a big guitar you've got there, mate.'

'It's not a guitar.'

'What is it then?'

'It's a double bass.'

'Wow. Did you hear that? I've never seen a double-bass guitar before.'

A New Romantic would just sit his keyboard on his lap and stare out of the window. No trouble, no hassle, just like any other passenger. The Bam on the Bus might be thinking lots of things about The New Romantic's choice of clothing, or taste in make-up, but there was something vaguely intimidating that would prevent even The Bam on the Bus from speaking up. It had been the same with the punks, although the reasoning was more obvious. If someone looks violent, they probably are violent. The Bam on the Bus's survival mechanism kicked in. Keep your mouth closed and hopefully they will get off soon.

The country and western brigade seemingly didn't invoke any such fear in The Bam on the Bus, even the ones leaving The Grand Ole Oprey carrying guns!

'What's the point in goin' hame on a bus when ye've goat a perfectly good horse parked outside?'

What was it about The New Romantics that made The Bam on the Bus leave them alone? Perhaps The New

Romantics posed such a conundrum that The Bam on the Bus didn't want to go there. Even in the 80s offence could easily be caused by assuming a male was a female and vice versa. It was OK to sit in your living room, with members of your family, watching Culture Club's first appearance on *Top of the Pops* and ponder, loudly, whether the lead singer was a man or a woman. But, on the whole, men wearing make-up were pretty rare.

I spent a lot of time on buses, mainly to avoid the Boundary Charge, and learned many a thing in the process. For example, it was The Bam on the Bus who informed me, and all the other passengers, that Pope John Paul II had been shot. Admittedly, a bit of prior knowledge of how The Bam on the Bus communicated was needed. Holding two fingers to the side of his head, saying 'El Papa', over and over again, and making a shooting sound at the same time was enough for those of us used to travelling with him.

***

Thankfully, we hadn't encountered The Bam on the Bus on the way to Buchanan Bus Station and the coast was still clear when we jumped on a corporation bus in George Square. When I say 'we', I mean me and JJB, my school pal and now partner in a burgeoning mobile disco venture. JJB was attending Glasgow College of Technology, studying something which involved wires, screwdrivers and the possibility of an electric shock. One of JJB's fellow students was an aspiring musician. He had a band – the type of band that could take their instruments on the bus. But no gigs.

JJB relayed to me a conversation that had taken place at college that week. The band were going to be rehearsing, had booked a venue and there was a possibility that we could get on the guest list. I felt a bit put out by this. Being DJs, we had the power to change the course of their future and the band should be grateful to have us there. I left it to JJB to make the arrangements with clear instructions that he should emphasise our importance within the music world.

The first surprise was the time of the gig. We would have to be up and out by 9am on Sunday morning to get there on time. The next surprise was the area we ended up in – barren, derelict, unpopulated. Not a church hall, theatre or community centre in sight. All I could see were bare bricks. If I looked far enough, there was a furniture showroom in the distance but we seemed to be walking away from it and towards... towards what? Had we been sold a bummer? Was this a wind up? I was anxious. JJB was calm. But I was sure we were walking towards a brick wall.

**

In my sheltered little life, it had never occurred to me that you could go inside a railway arch. I definitely never thought there could be a recording studio in such a place. But here I was, staring longingly at equipment I would have killed for, being introduced to people and not knowing what to expect.

The synthesised sound didn't surprise me in the slightest. If you spend all week with wires and screwdrivers and electric shocks, electropop is likely to be your route to fame. That's what everyone thought in the 80s. This lot were no different, but they were good. They weren't messing about and had a clear plan to get some tracks down on tape and to hawk them around in the hope of success. Struggling to catch up with what was going on around me, I had forgotten that was where JJB and I came in.

Luckily, JJB was ahead of me. A conversation had already taken place while I was in my trance. When we left this railway arch we would leave with a copy of the tape, we would promote it mercilessly, the band would become famous, we would be their managers and we would all live a luxurious life in which journeys on buses were a thing of the past.

***

The electropop hadn't taken me by surprise but *Hippy Hippy Shake* did! This band were cool. We were in the early stages of the electropop boom. What were they thinking? They wrote their own stuff and had belted it out for an hour or so and now this ancient song seemed to be the crowning glory. They must have had a vision. Madison Square Gardens with Depeche Mode supporting them. Crowds cheering, lead singer floating on the hands of an adoring public. The most recent worldwide best seller confidently despatched and the vocalist safely returned to the stage. The audience drooling for more. But always leave them wanting more, that was the old showbiz adage and it was just as true for The New Romantics as it was for the The Rat Pack. *Hippy Hippy Shake* for an encore? Give me a rest. This band needed management more than I had thought.

They kept getting it wrong, too. When the lead singer sang 'For goodness sake...', an electro beat was lined up to be brought in on the word 'sake'. Take 1 – the beat didn't come in at the right time. Take 2 – same again. Take 3 – singer starts with 'For goodness sake...' but in the wrong key. Take 4 – singer laughs uncontrollably before singing anything. Take 5 – wrong key again and on and on it went. The laughter was infectious. These guys just loved music and they weren't too moody to move away from their comfort zone. Secretly, neither was I. *Hippy Hippy Shake* had been part of my childhood, just like *Gangnam Style* would be for my children. The track wasn't coming together but the atmosphere in the railway arch was great, and it wasn't even lunchtime.

***

JJB and I left the railway arch clutching a cassette with four songs on it. *Hippy Hippy Shake* was not one of them. The standout track was called *Fear of God* and we played it every chance we got. I would love to conclude this by revealing that the band in question went on to become... But they didn't. And *Fear of God* never became a hit either. And JJB and I didn't become managers and continued using buses for a while longer.

For what it's worth, the band called themselves Earthworks. In the interests of clarity, another, more successful, band called Earthworks, a British jazz band led by Bill Bruford, came along a few years later. Originally, Bill Bruford's Earthworks featured a double bass in the line-up, but they dispensed with this. Too much hassle getting to gigs on the bus I suppose.

My Earthworks, if I can call them that, may not have made me rich but maybe they had hopes that I would do the same for them. Whatever the outcome, it was a fun way to spend a Sunday morning. After the session we tumbled out into the brightness of the street to look for the bus stop. Bare brick surrounded us everywhere, a reminder that the real world existed. We had learned something, though. Behind the bare brick, something wonderful might be going on. Please don't put yourself in danger but, if you get a chance, take a look inside. You might be pleasantly surprised.

KICK-OFF

At the same moment the referee blew his whistle to start the FA Cup Final replay, *The Concert* was scheduled to start at The Apollo. We were in The Ivanhoe. We had decided to take the calculated risk that The Stones would not start anywhere close to time. Rock 'n' Roll bands never did and this was The Greatest Rock 'n' Roll Band in the World.

There was the usual preamble. Get to The Ivanhoe in plenty of time, get the drinks in, join in Lonesome Dave's esoteric debate, settle down and watch as much of the match as we could and then head to The Apollo, probably at half-time.

The esoteric debate was more of a mini stand-up routine. Sadly, time has erased the two jokes that Lonesome Dave told but I remember eggs, Kit Kats and Joan Collins being mentioned. Three topics, but definitely only two jokes.

In the moments before kick-off, the FA Cup Final's finest tradition played out, the singing of *Abide With Me*. A hymn of hope in the darkest of times. Every year, without fail, it takes me by surprise and brings out the goose bumps. There is something strangely reassuring about 100,000 football fans preparing to vent bile at one another but coming together beforehand to sing a hymn. And then… let battle commence.

***

It was a beautiful, sunny night in Glasgow. Our minds weren't really on the game as much as they would normally have been. We kept checking watches and, the deeper we went into the first half, the more jittery we became. What if we got our timings wrong?

We reassured one another that staying until half-time would be comfortable. All you had to do was look at Keith Richards' face and you could tell that he probably didn't even get out of bed until after 7.30pm. There was no way he would be on stage until at least 9pm. Could we catch a bit of the second half? Too risky. The decision was made. We would leave at half-time, get to The Apollo and get into our seats in plenty of time. So that's what we did and, after making the short walk in the summer sunshine, we could see that some people were still arriving and no one was rushing. We had called it just right.

***

It was when we saw The Bouncer at the door that our plans took a handbrake turn. I wasn't sure how many beers we had had in The Ivanhoe but something made us feel that our luck might be in, that there might be more than just a gig to be had. The Bouncer wasn't on his own. Bouncers hunt in packs and there were a few of them milling around. Some of them looked over to see what the commotion was. The Bouncer signalled that everything was OK. We didn't realise how loud we were being but this was a once-in-a-lifetime opportunity. As our eyes adjusted to the artificial light of The Apollo's foyer our brains started thinking that this connection could make this night even more magical than we could ever have dreamed.

The conversation was cordial enough to start with. The Bouncer and I had never been friends as such but there had never been any disagreements, so we went through the cursory 'how are you doing' preamble and then started fishing for information. Were the band here? Yes they were. Would they be starting soon? It didn't look like it. Were they in their dressing room? Yes they were. Could The Bouncer get us in to meet them?

The Bouncer gave this some thought. This was encouraging. It occurred to me that we had been saying 'Mick and Keef' obsessively. Those were The Stones we really wanted to meet. No offence to the others, of course. But Mick and Keef. They were the ones.

The Bouncer asked us to wait for a minute and went to consult his colleagues. We stood muttering 'Mick and Keef' over and over again. We watched and tried to read the body language. Heads nodded. Glances were made in our direction. The pack needed convincing that we wouldn't blow this. If they were going to put themselves on the line it had to be with people they could trust. This was a risk.

The Bouncer broke away and headed back towards us.

'We need someone to do us a favour. Are you up for it?', he asked.

Were we up for it? This was the chance to meet Mick and Keef. We were up for anything. A bank job? You name it. If we get to meet Mick and Keef we're in.

***

The Bouncer motioned to us to follow him. We did so dutifully, still gibbering about Mick and Keef. The first part of the journey was familiar. We were entering the stalls. Our tickets were for upstairs. A seat in the stalls would be great. Could The Bouncer swing that too? This wasn't the time to ask.

We entered in near total darkness and there was music playing. What it was or who it was I have no idea. The Apollo was half full. These were the people who had done the decent thing. They had come to see the support. They hadn't abandoned their rock 'n' roll principles in exchange for 45 minutes of 22 men kicking a ball around Wembley. But they weren't going to meet Mick and Keef either!

The Bouncer led us down the aisle, stage left. At the end of the aisle there was a door, barely visible in the gloom. Were Mick and Keef through the door? Had someone gone on ahead and asked the band if four slightly drunk fans could meet them, even just for a few minutes? Maybe Mick had said 'well alright' straight away but Keef didn't want us coming into the dressing room.

'Bring them backstage, but not in here. Out in a corridor beside the beer crates. You sure they won't settle for Bill or Charlie?'

The Bouncer kept walking so we did too. We reached the door at the front of the auditorium. Audience members weren't allowed any further, but we weren't just any old audience members. The Bouncer pushed the door open. We followed him through. We were backstage at The Apollo! The gloom brightened, but only just. Still no sign of Mick and Keef.

We expressed disappointment but The Bouncer motioned to us to continue on with him. The corridors were dimly lit. There was no pretence of décor. The bare bricks were testament to that. We were in uncharted territory. We had no idea where we were going or which door Mick and Keef were behind. All we could do was trust our guide. The Bouncer kept walking so we kept following. The Bouncer opened a door and waved us through and we were blinded by the most almighty light that left us momentarily disorientated until we gradually began to focus.

GLASGOW IN MAY

If the title of this chapter was splashed across the front of a travel brochure, I don't imagine there would be a stampede. Paris in Springtime; New England in Fall. Those are the romantic notions that seduce travellers, but hear me out. If you are ever going to get decent weather in Glasgow, May is your month. It's a bit counter intuitive but I am sure it is true. Theoretically, June should be better but, if you have ever planned a relaxing Sunday lunch on the shores of Loch Lomond in June, you may have been treated to a view of fog, mist, harr, call it what you will. That's a pretty standard June in the west of Scotland.

There are exceptions of course but May comes up trumps more often than not and, when I think back to gigs in May, I think of warm sunshine streaming in windows while performers deliver acts that would normally take place in darkened theatres. I'm thinking of Mayfest, Glasgow's very own cultural arts festival. It was never intended to rival Edinburgh's Fringe but in its own way it brought the city alive and brought sights and sounds that might otherwise have gone unnoticed.

There would be ceilidhs in the Tramway and temporary grandstands were erected in the low end of Ruchazie for an open-air street performance. Theatre companies such as Clyde Unity and 7:84 mobilised themselves and toured the community centres of Govanhill, Wellhouse, Haghill and

Shettleston. Little old ladies, more accustomed to bingo, would be pushed out of their comfort zones by a particularly raunchy segment of *The Breadmakers Saga* and would make a great play of getting up from their seats, walking out and announcing to all and sundry that 'Ah'm no puttin' up wi' that.' The actors carried on as if nothing had happened.

It was the mid to late 80s. Mobile phones were still in brick form. Reminders had to be set manually. Ordering tickets was done from your landline or by turning up at the venue. Events were publicised in brochures and military-like precision was required to make sure you got the most out of Mayfest.

There were so many more shows to choose from than normal, with time-slots ranging from early evening to the small hours of the morning. Let me use the Renfrew Ferry as an example.

The first show would be at 6pm. The Ferry had to be cleared by about 8.30pm to let the audience in for the 9pm show. That lot had to be off by 11.30pm as there was another show at midnight. This opened up all sort of possibilities and I remember going to the 6pm show, straight from work, to see two upcoming young comedians. The sun streamed in the windows of The Ferry as Hattie Hayridge delivered her quizzical, whimsical observations on life before the stage was taken by storm by a young Jo Brand. She may write novels, make documentaries and host *The Great British Bake Off: An Extra Slice* now but when she burst onto the scene it was all double gussets, periods and cake. Oh, I see now that cake has been a constant theme throughout. But you didn't come away thinking about cake. You came away thinking about someone who was breaking the mould (not a cake mould), someone who was at the start of something we now see as normal.

There wasn't too long to dwell on that. There was just enough time to leave The Ferry, cross the river, get to Argyle Street, wolf down a pizza and return to The Ferry in time to see the aforementioned American blues legend Carey Bell as the sun finally set and The Ferry was enveloped in darkness.

**

Comedy was a big part of Mayfest. Comedians were on their way to becoming rock stars and filling huge arenas but they weren't quite there yet. That was no bad thing. Comedy needs intimacy. Comics need to connect with their audiences and smaller venues are better for that. Friday night had become TV comedy night. BBC 2 had a new panel show, *Have I Got News for You*. Channel 4 had *Cheers* at 9pm and *Rosanne* an hour later. You had to be cute with your VCR timer if you wanted to catch everything, especially if you were going out and planned to watch them when you came back. The other Friday-night unmissable was Channel 4's *Whose Line is it Anyway?* with Clive Anderson attempting to keep order in a format that was designed to do the opposite. *Whose Line is it Anyway?* brought the art of improvisation to UK screens. Paul Merton, Josie Lawrence, Mike McShane, Tony Slattery. They all became household names thanks to their ability to think on their feet and quickly construct a credible routine based purely on a word from or a whim of an audience member.

When I heard that The Comedy Store Players were coming to Mayfest I had to be there. We knew that Paul Merton and Josie Lawrence were part of The Players but we also knew that Paul Merton wouldn't be appearing in the Glasgow show. This was the 9 o'clock show on The Ferry and, as we sat waiting for it to start an announcement was made that Josie Lawrence would be unable to perform. There was an audible groan in the room before people returned to their conversations. A further announcement informed us that there were still tickets available for Fat Sam's Jazz Band who were on at midnight. There were no takers.

With Merton and Lawrence off the scene we didn't know what to expect but no one was disappointed. Tony Hawks (not the skateboarder) seemed to be in charge, or was it Neil Mularkey? It doesn't matter, and it didn't matter what the audience threw at The Players; they were consummate professionals and hilarious with it.

There must have been a break in proceedings because there was another announcement about tickets still being available for Fat Sam's Jazz Band at midnight. A quick scan of The Ferry told us that no one was buying tickets for that show; instead people were blowing into imaginary trumpets and saying 'hep cat' while Lonesome Dave mounted a fervent defence of jazz and tried to convince anyone who would listen that 'it wasn't all Kenny Ball and his Jazzmen'. He could rant and rave all he wanted. The Shugmeister had two young children who would be up at the crack of dawn and I was relying on him for a lift home – there was no way I was paying the Boundary Charge. Fat Sam's Jazz Band would just need to play to an empty Ferry and that was that.

The Comedy Store Players came back to the stage and worked their magic all over again. By the end of it everyone had forgotten who Paul Merton and Josie Lawrence were. No doubt their careers would go down the tubes.

The show finished and the announcements continued. 'Still tickets available' became 'discounted tickets available'. Most of the audience were heading for the exits. We were intending to do the same.

We were approaching the time when The Ferry would have to be cleared and we could see the jazz diehards, just a small band of them, queueing on the gang plank that led onto The Ferry, smoking in the way that only jazz diehards can.

'Ladies and gentlemen. Thank you for joining us on the Renfrew Ferry tonight. We hope you enjoyed the show and, as another show is due to commence soon, we have to ask you to finish off your drinks and move outside. Please take care on your way out and have a safe trip home.'

We started to say our goodbyes but there was a bit more.

'If anyone feels that the night is still young, let me remind you that we have another show this evening. Our midnight show features Fat Sam's Jazz Band and we are delighted to invite any of you who wish to stay to remain on The Ferry and join us as we work our way into the wee small hours.'

This was a game changer. A free show. Even if it was Fat Sam's Jazz Band. But we couldn't. It would be close on 2am before it finished. We couldn't. Could we?

I don't know who made the final decision but we were dancing by 12.30am and never stopped until Fat Sam's Jazz Band did. Lonesome Dave was right. Stick a bunch of performers on stage, let them do what they are good at and be prepared to let yourself go along with it. Your preference might be *The Breadmakers Saga* in Haghill or it might be Fat Sam's Jazz Band on the Renfrew Ferry. Whatever floats your boat!

THE THREE DOUGIES

There are some who would say Duggie and there are some who would say Doogie. Let's clear this up before we go any further. We are talking about the latter. Let's start with Dougie number one.

There has been a fair bit of talk about music and football so far and they apply in equal measure to Dougie number one. See how quickly you can work out which Dougie I am referring to.

He presented a late-night music show on Radio Clyde which once featured Lonesome Dave. He took over the Radio Clyde mid-morning show from its original presenter Steve Jones. He became BBC Scotland's football anchorman, introduced numerous editions of Grandstand and won/lost (delete as applicable) the commentators' lottery to describe the beach volleyball at the Olympics. This Dougie also became the snooker guy and the bowls guy.

Dougie number one is Dougie Donnelly.

Dougie number two is a musician who presented an evening blues show on Radio Scotland which featured Lonesome Dave on a number of occasions. This Dougie presented football on BBC Scotland and also became the bowls guy. Can you see a theme developing?

Dougie number two is Dougie Vipond.

Dougie number three, like Dougie number two, is a musician. To the best of my knowledge, he has no connection to snooker, bowls or beach volleyball. He does, though, have a football connection that I expect he would want to forget.

Dougie number three is Dougie MacLean.

***

Dougie Donnelly was the consummate professional. As well as appearing regularly on TV, Dougie was the go-to man for hosting functions, chairing discussions and seamlessly ensuring that awards ceremonies of all descriptions ran smoothly. Dougie's path and my path barely crossed – I admired his presentation skills from afar – but there was one day on which I could have reached out and touched him. I don't expect he would have appreciated me doing that.

The day in question saw an array of local bands booked to play outdoors in the bandstand in Kelvingrove Park. I have no recollection of which bands played but I was quite excited that Dougie Donnelly was going to be hosting. I skulked along on my own. I felt a bit sheepish and out of place so hung around like a bad smell on the outer edges of the seating area. When I got there Dougie was in the process of introducing the next act after which he left the stage. I pondered about what he might do in a situation like that. Did he go backstage and listen from the wings? Had he no interest in music and was broadcasting just a rung on the ladder to fame? Was he a music industry mogul looking for a band to represent that would make him a multi-millionaire?

I never got the answer to any of those questions but I did get the surprise of my life when Dougie Donnelly came into view. He marched up the steps towards where I was standing and then walked on into the distance. Maybe he was going for a 99. I will never know.

Some years later, I was asked if I would be willing to host the Miss Berlin beauty contest. It was sold to me on the basis that I would get to wear a dinner suit, 'you know, like Dougie Donnelly'. Thankfully the contest never took place and I was spared the embarrassment of having to say no.

***

Dougie Vipond gained the reputation of being hapless and accident prone thanks to the unpredictability of live TV. The *Only an Excuse* team played on this mercilessly but I think most people would agree that when *Only an Excuse* mocks someone mercilessly they do so from a place of warmth and affection.

Dougie Vipond won't remember me but I managed to blag my way into his Radio Scotland studio under the guise of 'supporting' Lonesome Dave. The backdrop was that Lonesome Dave had some stories to tell so, from time to time, he would contact people within the music industry and offload some of his tales. One day he will write them all down but for now we need to make do with an invitation to Dougie Vipond's *Blues & Soul Show* to talk about seminal drummers.

Dougie was charming, engaging, polite, meticulous and hugely knowledgeable. The two of them disappeared off into his studio for an entertaining 20 minutes while I sat listening on the other side of the glass. It was like Christmas morning for me. I was surrounded by more recording equipment than I had ever seen. This was like the Scotstoun railway arch multiplied by 100. I was sad when we had to leave.

There was nothing hapless about Dougie Vipond's drumming ability. Deacon Blue had a huge and loyal following in Scotland but they truly conquered the world, too. Those who chronicle the 80s will tell you that in the first half of the decade everyone had a copy of Dire Straits' 'Brothers in Arms' and that in the second half it was Simply Red's 'Stars'. This may be true but I have heard of many amicable separations turning sour when deciding who gets to keep 'Raintown'.

The SECC probably wasn't the best place to see Deacon Blue for the first time but it was a measure of their success that they could fill the place. It was another sunny night, perhaps in May and definitely in 1989. The venue was one of those one-size-fits-all places in which people in suits gather during the day to discuss electronic gadgets and ideal homes. It was never intended to provide perfect acoustics but that didn't really matter when you knew every song and could 'woo-ooo, woo-ooo' along with Ricky and Lorraine. We ended up dancing that Wednesday night away in a rooftop disco in Shawlands.

The second time I saw Deacon Blue was much more satisfying. Jim The Nipper was at the root of this. Jim The Nipper is a fan of silky soul but never lets a major event pass him by. In 1990 there were loads of major events in Glasgow as it was European City of Culture year, and Jim The Nipper and I attended a fair few of them. An exhibition in The Arches provided us with an old map of the city and we, naturally, zoned in on the places we had grown up – Roughazy and Queensleigh – as they originally appear to have been called when they were nothing more than farms. I was always saddened when people from other parts of the city had a dig at Ruchazie by rhyming it with 'crazy' which struck me as rather lazy. It seems that my discovery of its original name simply adds fuel to their fire.

One of the musical highlights of the year of culture was *The Big Day*, when everyone who was anyone, and Sheena

Easton, played at one of four locations across the city. Wet Wet Wet headlined George Square and we took in a bit of the action in the afternoon. Our main mission, however, was Glasgow Green in the evening and Big Country were in full flow when we arrived. The night couldn't fail after their set.

The place was packed and there was much anticipation about Deacon Blue at the top of the bill and boy did they deliver. Deacon Blue have lots of thoughtful, considered, intellectual songs but more than anything they have instantly recognisable anthems that play out brilliantly in a live setting. Glasgow Green was rocking as darkness fell and Dougie number two held the beat that drove every number.

I don't remember if we knew about the fireworks in advance or whether it came as a surprise, but Glasgow Green is the place to be for a fireworks display. People can talk about Disneyland, Sydney Harbour and The Birge Khalifa but if you come from Glasgow and you want fireworks head for Glasgow Green on 5 November. These days, wherever you go, your firework display will be choreographed. The introduction to Beethoven's fifth symphony will provide the anticipation to be followed by gentle flares lighting up the night sky as the string section gathers pace. This will give way to bangs, crashes and flashes to the sound of Dick Dale's *Misirlou* from the *Pulp Fiction* soundtrack. About three-quarters of the way through there will be a calmer section backed by The Verve's *Bitter Sweet Symphony*, giving the feeling that we are reaching the end before the crescendo explodes and ends perfectly in sync to Elgar's *Pomp and Circumstance*.

We didn't have choreographed fireworks displays in 1990. For me, getting to see some fireworks was good enough and, whether it was planned or whether it was luck, just as Ricky Ross counted the crowd into the 'stand it up' section, the fireworks exploded into the night sky. A few moments later, the music had come to an end and goodbyes were being said. The crowd hollered for more but there was still plenty going on in the sky. This was Glasgow, illuminated overhead and glowing warmly after a Very Big Day.

***

Dougie MacLean is a different kettle of fish from the other two Dougies. There won't be many people in Scotland who don't know Dougie MacLean and he is highly regarded in traditional music circles the world over. For many, though, the words 'traditional music' are enough to make them switch off. If I'm being honest, I was a bit like that myself for a while.

Traditional music for me meant Peter Morrison and Alasdair McDonald's *Songs of the North* on a Saturday night on BBC 1. I didn't go out of my way to watch it but it got in the way of *Sportscene* and seemed to have the capacity to make time slow down. It wasn't like that for my mother. She loved Peter Morrison's rich baritone as he sang of the Western Isles and the nooks and crannies of The Highlands. She laughed as Alasdair McDonald sang his little ditties about The Barras. She loved Kenneth McKellar too, and Moira Anderson and Jean Redpath, and spoke fondly of Johnny Beattie and *The White Heather Club*. When STV brought *Thingummyjig* to our screens she was beside herself.

Not so for me. Traditional music, accompanied by Scottish country dancing at school. No thanks, count me out.

I don't really know what changed but one day I woke up and traditional music didn't mean Peter Morrison and Alasdair McDonald any more. Country music didn't just mean Jim Reeves and Tammy Wynette. I didn't feel the need to shout 'yee-ha' if someone mentioned 'Bluegrass'. There was more to traditional music and what's more it appeared that it had been going all this time without me noticing. Tim and Mollie O'Brien, Tommy Sands, Karine Polwart, Mary Chapin Carpenter, Mary Coughlan, Alison Krauss. Where did they all appear from?

There were some things that shone through. The songs were important, the stories were important, the tradition was important. It was time to stop and listen to what the songs were about. English folk songs were no longer just about shipping disasters. Scottish folk music had much more depth than just providing the backing for a Canadian Barn Dance. Irish folk songs weren't just comedy numbers about pushing, shooshing and shoving a donkey.

There are some things you just don't get from a recording. Some things can only be fully understood when the artist explains what the song is about. Dougie MacLean is a singer-songwriter who sings songs that are personal to him. I had heard *Singing Land* being performed live and really enjoyed it but I had missed the introduction. I bought the CD and enjoyed listening to and singing along with the song. But I had no idea what it was about. That's why going to a gig is so important. Once Dougie explains the background, The Aboriginal people and the territories that were once theirs, the song takes on a new meaning. The plight, or the cause, that is behind the song comes to life and you hear it in a new light, but you can still sing along. It may be slow, melodic and haunting but there are few things more special than audience members in harmony with one another and singing something that means something, even if it is just in that moment.

It might have been Celtic Connections that got me started, but no, I don't think so.

Dougie MacLean at Cottiers stands out in my memory. On the one hand I questioned whether to go to the gig. The Shugmeister had been admitted to hospital that day. He was going through some tests and, when it was time to leave for the gig, we were none the wiser about the problem. It was unlikely to be anything serious but you never know. I decided to go to the gig. I wouldn't be out for that long but, with all of the indecision, we were cutting it neat. We got there just in time and the place was full. We took our chances and looked for a seat near the front. There was a single seat in the front row and one at the end of the second. I took that one and barely noticed the man on my right.

The first half passed off without incident. The interval came and lots of people, including the man to my right, nipped off to the bar. The second half started up and the audience were in raptures at the thoughtful lyrics and fine musicianship on display. From time to time, the music went a bit upbeat but, more often than not, Dougie would be singing a poignant tale of Highland clearances or unrequited love. That's why the snoring was becoming a bit of a problem.

I take it my neighbour for the night had had one too many and, with the melodious tunes lulling everyone into mesmerised admiration, it was easy to see how someone 'under pressure' could just nod off. Thankfully, his snoring didn't carry too far and we were spared Dougie giving the audience a telling off, as I once saw him do in a tent at a festival where the bar was at the back off the room and those less interested in his offerings were refreshing themselves and chatting to their mates. My neighbour didn't incur Dougie's wrath but did over-compensate each time a song finished and, as the applause woke him up, he performed the classic drunken response of clapping loudly, cheering and pretending he had never been asleep at all. Once the appreciation died down and Dougie started on the next number my friend would drift off and repeat the process throughout the rest of the gig.

Once Dougie had said his goodbyes and the audience had started gathering bags and jackets I caught, in the corner of my eye, my companion stretching, yawning and looking at me as if to say, 'I wonder if anyone noticed.'

'Did you enjoy that?' I asked. It was the best I could come up with.

'F*****g brilliant!'

***

Dougie's brush with football came on the Renfrew Ferry one sunny Wednesday night in May. If it had taken place 24 hours later, it would have coincided with the 27th anniversary of the night I was blinded by that bright light on my way to meet Mick and Keef. But it had to take place on a Wednesday because that's the night Radio 2's *Folk Show* goes out.

It seemed like a good idea at the time. Dougie MacLean, Capercaillie and an unremembered artist were playing live on the show, which lasted one hour and then, after an interval, the shackles were off and the acts would come back on stage to wow the audience some more. Sounds great, but there was a slight problem caused by Manchester United reaching the Champions League Final against Bayern Munich in Barcelona. I quite fancied seeing that.

The internet didn't yet have its massive reach so I set the video recorder and toddled off to The Ferry having finally worked out that one-off experiences like this had to be grabbed, whereas even the Champions League Final could be caught up on, even if it did mean a very late night. With a bit of luck I might even avoid the score.

***

A radio show featuring live music, in a venue I love, is somewhere close to my idea of heaven. But radio shows have to be tight. There wasn't a lot of time for rambling stories about the meaning or origin of the songs. The first hour was perfunctory; professionals at work. Very nice, thank you.

The radio show finished and that signalled the interval for those of us on The Ferry. Mike Harding thanked everyone for coming along, and behaving, during the live broadcast and explained that the talent would be back soon. Before climbing onto his motorbike and driving back to Rochdale he mentioned that Bayern Munich were leading 1-0 at half-time. Hmmm... Maybe I could just watch the second half when I got home. I would get to bed a bit earlier. Yes, that would work.

***

Capercaillie were top of the bill. The unremembered act came on first – someone Irish? Dougie was next. He launched into his storytelling and seduced the audience with lots of references to Gaelic. I was ahead of most people on this. I had already heard Dougie talking of his love for Lewis, the time he spent there, his attempts to learn the language and the locals tolerating him for being a trier.

The song, when it came along, was haunting, but that doesn't really do it justice. It was mesmeric, but that seems overused and inappropriate. It was melodic, but that seems a little too plain.

Sfhada Leam An Oidche Ghemhraidh

On paper it means nothing but, for the audience on The Ferry, we could have been drifting on the waters around the Western Isles. Dougie MacLean, playfully mocked on the islands for his pigeon version of the language, was making time stand still as we sat, in awe at this beautifully constructed, indecipherable love song which somehow we understood. Perfection captured between one man and his guitar. That's when the first shout came from below deck.

It was the most inopportune moment you could have imagined. An audience, collectively entranced and then, suddenly, jolted out of their reverie. What could have happened? Who would do such a thing? Not a music lover, surely?

Dougie continued like the true professional he is. Unfazed, he strummed and he sang. We tried to return to the place he had taken us. The tune, the melody, the strange foreign-sounding words of our forefathers. We were drifting again. The island was coming back into sight. A simpler life was beckoning. And that's when the second shout came from below.

Dougie rounded off his song. We applauded. We stood. We cheered. We had just witnessed a master at work. You wouldn't even have known that Dougie had noticed. He seemed to be totally transfixed by his song. But he had noticed and he wasn't happy about it and the radio broadcast was over so he was free to say whatever he wanted.

There were no expletives but there was admonishment just the same. He said something about people working on The Ferry with TVs below deck and muttered disdainfully about whether football was so important that it should get in the way of beautiful music.

***

As we waited for Capercaillie to take to the stage I pondered what those shouts might mean. They hadn't sounded like out-and-out cheers but there was some form of excitement attached to them. Had they been Manchester United goals, or near misses, or groans? I still didn't actually know the final score so watching the second half at home was still an option.

Capercaillie took to the stage and they simply don't do bad gigs. They blew us all away with one or two numbers to get things kicked off. Karen said 'Hello' and prepared to launch into another but there was an announcement to be made first of all. An announcement by a sheepish band member who had been sitting below deck watching TV, watching his beloved Manchester United eclipse Bayern Munich with football's most enthralling comeback ever. Unfortunately, the goals had been scored right in the middle of Dougie's haunting Gaelic ballad. Of course he had cheered. It was just a pity about the timing.

He apologised but didn't say what the score was. I had heard two cheers. Did that mean that United had won? Or had they just taken it into extra-time? One cheer for the goal, one for the final whistle. I suppose that could make sense.

Capercaillie made me forget about football for a while. When I got home I started to fast-forward. No point in watching the first half and, judging by the timing of the cheers, there was little point in watching most of the second half either. I wound on to 85 minutes, hit pause and clicked on the kettle. Once I got settled, I would watch the equaliser and then, maybe, the extra-time.

I sat down to enjoy my tea. There's the equaliser – Sheringham. Now what? Surely it must be extra-time. The final whistle was just about to blow but Ole Gunnar Solskjær had other ideas. The Bayern Munich players sat, dejected, the Manchester United players celebrated and I got to bed at a sensible time after all.

THE SECOND HALF

Being blinded by a very bright light is no fun but my eyes started to focus eventually. I could see the familiar bare brick of The Apollo's walls but no superstar rock stars were homing into view. All I could see was The Bouncer and he was pressing something into my hand.

'Where's Mick and Keef?' I drawled as reality dawned.

This wasn't The Rolling Stones' dressing room. This was the lane at the back of The Apollo. We had been brought in, and taken straight back out, into the evening sunlight. I realised The Bouncer was holding my hand and I felt slightly uneasy. I pulled my hand away and found I was holding money. The Bouncer was speaking. He wanted us to do him a favour. I wasn't sure if I fancied this. He had just double-crossed me. Just like he had five years ago with the girl of my dreams. He had told us we were going to meet Mick and Keef. Or had he? I remembered him saying something about helping him out. Surely that meant if we scratched the bouncers' backs they would scratch ours. But he hadn't actually said that we were going to get to meet Mick and Keef.

'Get us a bottle of Smirnoff. We're not allowed to drink when we're on duty so don't let anybody see it when you come back. The off sales shuts at nine.'

'Will we get to meet Mick and Keef when we come back?'

I think we knew we wouldn't but at least we had been reassured that there was still a bit of time before The Stones took to the stage. Perhaps there would even be enough time to go back to The Ivanhoe to check on the score. We went through a number of thoughts. *Nip round to The Ivanhoe just to check on the score and don't have a drink. Maybe have a drink. At all costs, don't miss the off sales. Maybe three of us could have a drink and the other one could go to the off sales.*

Somehow, we pitched back up at The Apollo and smuggled the Smirnoff in but a bit too conspicuously for The Bouncer's liking. That's what he gets for trusting four very drunk idiots who struggled to choose between the FA Cup Final and The Greatest Rock 'n' Roll Band in the World. We must have got away with it because our reward was an upgrade from our crappy seats in the gods to a place in the stalls, just in time for Mick, Keef and the boys to take to the stage.

Jagger was wearing a Scotland top, apparently. I don't remember that but folklore tells of England footballers in the audience and Jagger wearing a Scotland top on stage. We were, after all, less than 48 hours away from the annual clash between The Auld Enemy at Hampden.

No one sat. No one stood. Everybody danced. We were in The Apollo and The Greatest Rock 'n' Roll Band in the World were on stage, right in front of us, doing what they do. We danced in the aisles to numerous Stones classics and a fair few cover versions. *Going to a Go-go* was the new single and The Big Bopper's *Chantilly Lace* took us by surprise but not half as much as The Temptations' *Just My Imagination (Running Away With Me)*. If only I had remembered what I learned at The Commodores' gig. For every *Machine Gun* there is a *Three Times a Lady*.

Our problem was that our upgrade didn't amount to a *seat* in the stalls. Just *getting into* the stalls. As soon as a slow song came on The Shugmeister and I were horribly exposed. I have no idea where the other two went.

There was no sign of The Bouncer and none of the other bouncers looked familiar from our earlier encounter. The only ones on duty in this part of The Apollo had their serious heads on. Maybe they weren't in on the smuggled Smirnoff. We didn't dare ask. Didn't want to get anyone into trouble.

We had to show our tickets. Conversation was impossible because of the noise but the sign language was clear. We couldn't be here. Fingers pointed upwards and off we went, high on football, alcohol and rock 'n' roll. We needed to get to the gods quickly before we missed anything.

THREE FOR ONE AT
THE BARRAS

On one of my earliest trips to The Barras the mission was to buy a Mother's Day gift. It was a Sunday and my dad took me as we wanted it to be a surprise. The traders were in full flow in the streets. Carpets, teddy bears, bingo, food. Anything that existed could be bought there. I was more taken by the indoor areas. Lines of stalls, undercover, heaving with people and surely a repository for the world's entire supply of bric-a-brac. We coursed up and down the aisles, the crowds weaving to avoid me, the small boy, oblivious to everyone else and agog at the array of stuff on view.

I was particularly drawn to a small calendar. Imagine a globe of the world. Now imagine placing it on a work surface and flattening it with the palm of your hand, just as you would if you wanted to turn a large meatball into a small burger. Next, mount the burger vertically on a small plinth. Both sides of the burger have little cut-outs on them to make a calendar. One for the day, one for the date and one for the month. If the side you are looking at says Thu, 27 May all you have to do is rotate it 180 degrees and you will magically see Fri, 28 May. I knew immediately that my mum would love this. I knew this for certain because, on the day I visited The Barras, the visible side was showing Wed,

25 Jan which, as we established earlier is the shared birthday of Stewpot, Big Hendy, Robert Burns and me. How could she fail to like it?

From that day on, The Barras never disappointed. I would return time and time again, initially with my dad, but later with JJB for a Sunday raid on the ex-jukebox records that didn't have any middles. I was keen to expand my collection. I had made reasonable progress since buying *My Sweet Lord* and *The Pushbike Song* but the thirst was becoming unquenchable. The Barras was a place in which you could pick up major hits for 10p and my collection blossomed thanks to this most unique market place.

***

The Barras should not be confused with The Barrowland but often is, and I got one of the greatest bargains of my life at The Barrowland, I think.

I was told The Heilan' Jessie was the perfect place to start things off. I had no idea what the protocol was because it took me until the mid-80s to attend a Barrowland gig. My parents had reminisced about its days as a dance hall and my friends had raved about who they had seen there. For me it was all a bit of a mystery, a new experience, the wrong end of town for someone whose bus pulled into Killermont Street. Most of my shopping was done in Sauchiehall Street. Only if Marks and Spencer didn't have my size would I trudge down to Argyle Street and seldom any further. When I did go to The Barras I approached from the Duke Street end. The Barrowland was in a no man's land where I never seemed to tread. When the time finally came for me to go there I just did what I was told. Lonesome Dave was in charge. The Heilan' Jessie was the appointed meeting place and all I had to do was turn up and follow instructions.

Please don't groan when I name the first act. Most people do but this lot weren't always groan-inducing. There was a time when they stuck pretty close to the roots of soul before they knocked Dire Straits off their perch and took residency on the coffee tables of penthouse flats across the UK. The curse of *Bo' Selecta* had not yet ripped their credibility away and foppish red hair and the ability to hit soprano-like notes were still seen as positive attributes. Simply Red were, at that time, just about to burst onto the scene. *Money's Too Tight (To Mention)* was creeping up the charts and Mick Hucknell's vocal ability had to be heard to be believed. The Barrowland was mobbed and we bobbed up and down, being careful not to spill any of the beers we held in each hand.

This was part of The Barrowland ritual that I would come to learn. Venues like The Apollo were unlicensed so you could have a beer before the show but not during it. This was no bad thing, as you could concentrate on the show, standing or seated, depending on who was singing what. Things were different in The Barrowland. It was standing only and I seem to remember makeshift bars, basically tables, where you could buy drinks. No one wanted to force their way through the crowd and lose their vantage point so it was customary to buy as many beers as you could hold, find a spot near the stage and take in the show without having to move. It did make clapping a bit difficult so stamping a foot on the floor was one way of showing appreciation, along with the normal whoops, hollers and whistles that you would expect. Lonesome Dave had his own method. 'Yahoo!' he would shout. 'Oh, Yahoo!'

As far as I could tell, Simply Red were here to deliver a much-needed dose of raw soul to the disciples who attended that night. I wasn't aware they had heart-throb status and I didn't expect the groupies at the end of the night. But as we were making our way from The Barrowland into the Glasgow night a vehicle emerged. It must have been carrying the band judging by the screaming girls clawing at the door handles and the windows. One hit and the world is your oyster.

***

Simply Red were on the way up. Big enough to sell tickets in their own right but still a support act when it came to the big hitters. So where did they fit in relation to the next act? The Robert Cray Band hit the UK and hit me fairly and squarely between the eyes. Lonesome Dave was in charge of musical introductions and I just did what I was told. I was learning that you didn't have to be a household name to be successful and have a big following. TV programmes such as *The Tube* and *The Whistle Test* would showcase bands who came to the UK but perhaps hadn't come to the attention of all. Often these acts would be top-of-the-range practitioners in their own field, or country, and a bit of exposure would sell more tickets and the album sales would follow.

The Robert Cray Band contained some of the finest exponents of blues you could ever wish to see. Robert Cray himself possessed a B.B. King-like ability on guitar and I marvelled as we watched his band over the bobbing heads of the crowd around us. There was much foot-stamping and many 'Yahoos!' while The Robert Cray Band graced The Barrowland stage. I was trying to keep track of the lyrics. There was something about the words that this guy was singing. These were not 'my woman dun gone left me' blues songs. The guitar sound, which would have won awards in its own right, was an accompaniment, no, a complement, to the dark, sardonic humour contained within the lyrics of songs about the deepest feelings of human beings. This was Grammy Award-winning music. We knew that before we went and now we could tell why.

Simply Red were on the way up. The Robert Cray Band were already big in the States but not yet in the UK. The band had already made their mark and legions of people around the world were following. Now, in a small corner of my city, a new crop of followers were being inducted.

Did I buy the album? I will treat that question with the contempt it deserves. How can someone take the break-up of relationships, or maybe even adultery, and express all of the raw emotion and destruction that go with those things while still delivering killer pay-offs? I won't quote them. If you've never heard The Robert Cray Band go and find them.

***

We have established that Simply Red were the support act and that, although The Robert Cray Band were not widely known in the UK at the time, they were big enough to merit a slot further up the bill. So who would the headline act be? This is where being Scottish helps.

A phenomenon hit music in 1987 and it was a phenomenon that originated in this wonderful country. From time to time an artist or a group come along and what they do is so unbelievably different from anything that has been done before that they don't just occupy a space in time, they claim that space forever. No one was going around saying that we needed this because no one knew that it existed. Someone somewhere must have heard them. That person must have spread the word. Even without Facebook, Twitter and all the rest, the word got out and a recording contract was agreed. Their music didn't fit into a genre. It wasn't something that would be play-listed because no one knew what it was. But there was something, wasn't there? You could dance to it. You could waltz to it. It could make you cry. It could make you laugh. It could make you angry. And then there were the accents.

Most Scottish bands sing in American accents. The word Scottish could be removed from the previous sentence and it would still hold true. But this band sang in Scottish accents. Broad Scottish accents. There was something comical about the voices. The way they blended together. The way one voice sang one line and another voice sang the next. There was something about the music that complemented the words perfectly. There was something about the words and how they captured the emotion of the song. There was something about the amount of blood, sweat and tears that had clearly gone into the writing that quickly took you beyond the accents, quickly took you beyond the appearances. The comical aspect was swiftly forgotten and your focus turned to the unemployed, the displaced, the disenfranchised and those treated with contempt by their healthier, wealthier paymasters.

The Proclaimers ripped up the script and wrote their own. They hit the ground running and before you knew it they were everywhere. And here they were, top of the bill, playing just for me – and numerous others – at The Barrowland. Had I known how good they would be, how accomplished, how entertaining, how professional, I would have forgone the two pints, one in each hand, so that I could clap. Foot-stamping and even shouts of 'Yahoo!' didn't do this justice. The Proclaimers were hot property and they were Scottish so they had to be top of the bill. Maybe when they went on tour in America they would open for a headline act but they would place that headline act in the greatest show business conundrum of all. How do you follow that?

***

Everything you have just read is just about true but there is an insinuation that doesn't really hang together. Simply Red's *Money's Too Tight (To Mention)* hit the UK charts in 1985. Robert Cray came to the UK in 1987 and The Proclaimers broke through later that year. By that time, Simply Red were at the top of their game and well past the stage of opening for the other two. Yet in my mind it was one gig that took place on one night. If it had, it would be difficult to explain how I managed to go to The Heilan' Jessie before each band. Or how I was with different friends depending on which band was on stage. Or how I saw those girls, clawing at Simply Red's vehicle after their gig, given that I would have been watching The Robert Cray Band or The Proclaimers at the time. It would have finished late, too and that would have taken me into Boundary Charge territory. Not something I agreed to willingly.

On reflection, there must have been three different gigs on three different nights, but that's The Barras for you. Smoke and mirrors and you leave believing you got a bargain.

THE ANTIPODEAN HUMPFF

When Kylie and Charlene touched down in the UK, a traditional Scottish welcome awaited them. After such a long journey, they would need rest, sustenance and time to familiarise themselves with their surroundings. Or so we thought. It transpired that they just needed a day or so and then they were out in Glasgow as if they had lived here all their lives. Once they knew the places to go, like most Australians, they didn't need an invitation to make themselves feel very much at home.

Kylie and Charlene were young, full of energy, devoid of fear and threw themselves into everything that Glasgow had to offer. I enjoyed watching their culture bounce against ours and was never disappointed with the outcome. They embraced the nightlife and the music, but they embraced their family connections too and it was an experience for all of us who were in some way connected to them.

I suppose if I went to Sydney, I wouldn't have preconceived ideas about this or that part of town. That's how it was for Kylie and Charlene. Home became a flat in Garthamlock and their local became The Town Tavern in Shettleston. The Shugmeister felt a unique sense of responsibility towards them, having promised their parents to look after them when they were so far away from home. His task was like herding cats and that's where The Humpff Family came in.

***

The Humpff Family were a band I would struggle to describe. Scottish folk-a-billy seems to be the closest anyone has ever got. But there was a chaos about them, they were an unruly mob with an anarchic twist, had an insatiable energy and a flagrant disregard for the rules. I want to say there was a guy playing a tea chest but it may actually have been a double-bass guitar, as The Bam on the Bus would say. There was something about teaching Jeasus, not Jesus, how to swim, but I can't elaborate any further on that as you will find out. There were albums and TV appearances, local tours and world tours. There was critical and popular acclaim. There were accolades by the truck load but none of what has just been said does justice to the reputation the band carved out for itself. The Shugmeister knew this and used it as part of his masterplan to get Kylie and Charlene out and partying where they could be kept under his watchful eye.

Where they first saw The Humpff Family I will never know because I wasn't there. All I know is that they came back converted and that their lives would never be the same again. This was a band I had to see.

***

Fast-forward to The Riverside Club and one of many legendary ceilidhs. Kylie and Charlene are there and I'm intrigued to get to know the real people behind the cheesy updates that ex-pats send back home in the run-up to Christmas. Every year, for who knows how long, we were told of success after success. Top class degrees, house moves, swimming pools, job promotions. Was there nothing they couldn't do? Admittedly, there was never any mention of the cannabis plants that brother Jason had been growing in the garden at home, and that his mother had been watering in blissful oblivion, but no one wants to spoil Christmas, do they?

The real Kylie and Charlene, not the caricatures, were here, immersing themselves in Scottish culture, attending a ceilidh, a proper one, for the first time. I could see that it didn't take them long to catch on. I watched them birling and whirling. No mean feat when I, too, was birling and whirling at a rate of knots.

Ceilidhs at The Riverside placed high expectations on the bands who provided the soundtrack to the evening. It was no longer good enough just to play the traditional tunes. The bands wouldn't be invited back unless they could differentiate themselves from the plethora of others that populated the ceilidh scene. Quirky names became all the rage but quirky music featured too. A Dashing White Sergeant may start in traditional Jimmy Shand mode. That's what gets people on the floor, but then it would deviate. Maybe there would be a traditional take on a well-known tune. It took a while to work it out. Was it The Beatles? No, Wet Wet Wet? Can't be. That would be ridiculous. Rock Around The Clock? And by the time you got slightly closer to identifying the mystery piece it had deviated off into something classical, played on fiddles, accordions and drums. If the band were particularly accomplished, they would go off on tangents from all musical genres. Some lend themselves better than others. Ceilidh bands the world over will struggle to play Motorhead or AC/DC, but traditional music weaves its tentacles in all sorts of directions and, before you knew it, Jimmy Shand gave way to Skiffle and Bluegrass and then we were on for a hoedown. The crowd picked up the rhythm and the whoops and hollers grew louder and louder. Hands, when they could be detached from partners, added to the throng with thunderous clapping sounds and the 'hoochs' and 'choochs' from this part of the world became the 'yee-has' from many thousands of miles away across the water. In fact, a perfect accompaniment to Humpff Family dancing.

No one noticed at first but Kylie and The Shugmeister had gone off on their own. As people began to catch on they stopped dancing to watch. What they saw were two people, lost in a world of Humpff-ness, tucking actual thumbs into imaginary dungarees and prancing back and forth, meeting each other in the middle, backing off, approaching again, passing one another, do-si-do style, and then repositioning themselves to face each other before backing away to start the ritual again.

The Riverside was in uproar. Everyone had stopped dancing. Only the band continued as the entire crowd formed a human circle and Kylie and The Shugmeister strutted, dipping at the knees, bowing to one another, shoulders bobbing up and down, as the human circle clapped and cheered and the band played on.

The two of them must have been tired. They had been going for a while but the wave of enthusiasm that swept the room was infectious. This completely impromptu, improvised performance was turning into the highlight of the night. People roared and cheered. The band played on. Kylie and The Shugmeister quenched their thirst on the atmosphere in the room and went for it one more time. Thumbs, shoulders, knees. Feet splayed to the side. Waddling back and forth towards each other and away again. Another approach and this time they passed. Back to back they crossed over and reversed to where they had started. They exchanged a knowing look. In some telepathic, Humpff-induced, communication they decided to go for a big finish. The thumbs were still in the dungarees. The knees were still bent. But now the knees were bending more. All the way down and back up again. The band were still playing but they must have needed a break. If the band needed a break how must Kylie and The Shugmeister feel? But still the knees bent, down and back up. Thumbs never left their position and bodies maintained the manic shoulder movements that brought authenticity to the routine. The knees were bending again but this time not straightening. This was the last hurrah, the crescendo. The knees stayed bent and Kylie and The Shugmeister stayed down, facing one another, instinctively knowing that this had to end and that the end must be worthwhile. Their intuitive minds spoke to one another. The congregation whooped and hollered and yee-hahd and wondered what to expect. Kylie and The Shugmeister began to kick their legs. The thumbs were still in the dungarees. The shoulders were still bobbing, one after the other. There was nothing to hold them but gravity but they went for it like Cossacks. Such a shame that The Shugmeister fell on his arse!

It had to end sometime. It was a pity it ended the way it did but it didn't matter. The punters at The Riverside had value for money that night and roared their appreciation. The band decided to have a break. If it hadn't been for The Humpff Family none of that would have happened. I had to see this band.

***

I'm at The Fleadh on Glasgow Green. When we arrive, Dougie MacLean is playing on the main stage. This type of setting doesn't lend itself to Dougie's storytelling style but there are enough of his fans here to make sure his talents are appreciated, and there are no tense, last-minute finishes to football matches to interrupt his sensitive ballads.

Everyone has brought a picnic. It seems that we have brought a better picnic that the others. Pin wheel smoked salmon bites and freshly prepared strawberries. We make the mistake of offering them around and they are gone in an instant. The others share their picnics with us but we can't help feeling that we got the thin end of the Camembert.

It is time to make a decision. Van Morrison is playing the main stage and, at the exact same time, The Humpff Family are playing in a tent. I can't be in two places at once. I have never seen Van Morrison and he is a legend. This might be my only chance. But I have never seen The Humpff Family either. I want to see for myself what they are all about.

I wander around for a while. I am outside The Humpff Family tent but I am not far from the main stage. I hover. I dither. I prevaricate. Some of our crowd are going to see The Humpffs. Some are going to see Van the Man. What should I do? I need to make a decision.

I don't regret choosing Van Morrison. I didn't know if the chance would ever come along again. As it turns out, it did, but a legend is a legend and, even in the 90s, Van was getting on a bit and you just couldn't tell when he might decide to bark, grouchily, at his band for the last time.

As soon as Van finished I made my way to the tent. Maybe I could catch the end of The Humpff Family's set. As I walked towards the tent I could swear it was moving. The thrashing noise that came from inside made it seem like the tent could take off at any moment. I walked faster and inched closer. And then the music stopped and loud cheers rang out. There were muffled sounds of voices through microphones and happy faces emptied themselves out of the tent, some with thumbs in imaginary dungarees.

It looked like a good time was had by all. I had to see this band.

***

Over Christmas I created an imaginary nightclub in honour of Kylie and Charlene, The Sydney Apollo, a feeble excuse to force a group of people to do a party piece on a Karaoke machine that someone had been given by Santa. I donned my best cod-Australian accent, took on the mantle of MC and berated everyone into performing. Australians don't really need to be berated. Everyone joined in and we were set fair for another six months of merriment. Early in the New Year word came through that Kylie and Charlene's parents, Bruce and Edna, were coming to Scotland. Brother Jason was coming too.

We heard about The Humpff Family gig around the same time as the surprise party. Coincidentally, they would both take place in The Wellshot Halls in Shettleston, The Humpff Family on the Friday and the surprise 50th on the Saturday. The party was for Edna and we were all sworn to secrecy and given our tasks to make sure the night went with a bang.

Tickets for The Humpff Family were purchased and arrangements were made. The gig had an early start so we had to be out super early and The Heilan' Jessie was the designated meeting place at 4pm. I got away from work early and had already discharged my duties for the surprise 50th. I had been asked to bake the birthday cake thanks to a successful attempt at the Christmas cake we had all munched on when we pretended to be in The Sydney Apollo. Christmas cakes have to be made weeks in advance and fed with booze, so I had handed it over in good time and was free to relax and enjoy myself.

It seemed a bit strange that the surprise 50th had been arranged for the day after Bruce, Edna and Jason stepped off the plane but there you have it. I suppose they must have wanted the party as close to Edna's birthday as possible. And as if that wasn't enough, Jason would be stepping off a plane from the other side of the world and being dragged immediately into an alien world to see a chaotic, unruly, anarchic mob in an unusual setting. Poor boy.

Those of us who were first to arrive at The Heilan' Jessie sat back and enjoyed a drink and a catch up. Phone calls were made. The plane had arrived on time. The travellers had been picked up and had been fed and watered. Jason would be joining us soon and, when he arrived, his sisters, naturally, showered him with affection. We then got a chance to be introduced properly and I felt it was my duty to provide warm Scottish hospitality. I offered him a pint. There was a decent choice of beers available. I figured he would want to sample the local brew. He asked if they had any Bourbon. I should have known there and then.

The Shugmeister was meeting us later. He would want to chaperone Jason but, until he got here, that would be my job. I kept an eye on Jason. He didn't seem shy and it looked like he had moved beyond our company and was making new friends. Had he no idea? Glasgow is a great place, but it can be a dangerous place. I stayed close, bought him the occasional drink. He bought me one back. Seemed like a nice guy.

By the time we got to The Wellshot Halls Jason seemed more at home in my city than I have ever been. He had linked up with various hangers on and spent a lot of time in the toilets, laughing and cavorting mostly, but hurriedly concealing whatever it was he was up to whenever anyone appeared. For some reason I was beginning to feel the night slipping away, along with my faculties. Thank goodness The Shugmeister had arrived. He could look after Jason now… and maybe me too.

Somehow, I never did get to see The Humpff Family that night. I'm pretty sure Jason did.

***

Some people had cooked, others had baked, some had decorated the hall, someone had organised the band and someone had made a Christmas cake for a 50th birthday party in April. That same someone struggled to drag himself to The Wellshot Halls that night but made it just the same. It's what you do, isn't it?

Edna, the birthday girl, who had stepped off the plane just 24 hours earlier, did her best when she was told she was being taken out when she would rather have slept. She did even better when she walked into a room and saw dozens of friends, family, loved ones and hanger-oners cheering, popping streamers and belting out *Happy Birthday to You*. It must have been a lot for her to take in.

Kylie and Charlene gave credit to everyone who had made it possible. My Christmas birthday cake got a special mention. Everyone was thanked for their efforts, especially as it was a surprise. The only thing that wouldn't have come as a surprise to Edna was that Jason spent most of the night in the toilet.

***

Once the Aussies were back on the other side of the world, a video started doing the rounds. It captured the highlights of Bruce and Edna's trip although 'highlights' might not do it justice. Bruce's tendency to film everything that ever happened meant that it was a forensic record of their time in Scotland to show the folks back home.

We sat down to relive happy memories but it seemed that all we were watching was a car journey down the M8. The car was travelling west and the camera's view was straight out of the front windscreen on the passenger side. The picture became darker as the car went into the short tunnel just before the Kingston Bridge and then we were going up and over and back down on the south side of the river. The lens was picking up a fairly wide shot but it was just road, cars, white lines and road signs. I didn't need someone to send me this footage from Australia. I saw it every day of my life. We stopped watching, perplexed. We must have been given the wrong video. I checked with The Shugmeister. It was the correct video. Apparently the ex-pat Scots back in Sydney just love seeing the road signs. The Aussies were heading to Burns Cottage on the day of filming and they knew that their neighbours and friends back in Sydney would be dewy eyed as they barbecued shrimps after seeing names like Maybole and Tarbolton flashing past.

Now that we had a clearer idea of what we were dealing with, it came as no surprise when the next section of the video cut, *Psycho*-like, to the kitchen units in The Shugmeister's new house. Whether this was of interest to the residents of Sydney or whether it was just part of Bruce's obsession I'm not sure, but at least we knew what we were dealing with. It came as something of a relief when the video cut to happier scenes. Here was Edna arriving at The Wellshot Halls. Everyone was poised for her arrival. She walked in the door and was taken aback as the surprise was sprung, and the memories came flooding back of the time the Aussies had been with us. The video came to an end and we were left with that moving, crackling, grainy, black-and-grey image that signified that there was no more footage on the tape. We sat back, smiling, remembering The Sydney Apollo, the surprise party, The Riverside ceilidh, and all the other nights we had spent with our visitors.

But the video wasn't quite finished after all. The grainy picture disappeared and we turned to see what was next. In most videos this would be the remnants of a film now taped over. It was Edna, talking to the camera and looking for all the world as though it was something she did on a daily basis. Maybe it was.

We worked out that she had filmed this for her neighbours back home. We didn't know if this was how they always communicated but it looked like a 50th birthday celebration had been arranged before she left for Scotland and this was her saying thanks. The footage had obviously been deemed surplus to requirements with worktops and road signs taking precedence.

'… going to Scotland… girls are already there… Jason is coming with us… will be great to see the family…'

Nothing to see here, but we kept watching because it just seemed a little bit odd.

'… love Robert Burns… will make a point of going to his cottage… will miss you all… will update you when we get back…'

Time to switch off?

'… girls have arranged a party for my 50th… don't want anyone to make a fuss… but they insist…'

What? That was supposed to be a surprise!

***

Surprise or not, I would have baked the Christmas birthday cake anyway. The hall would have been decorated. The food would have been prepared. The party poppers would have been popped. Why did they feel the need to pretend it was a surprise?

I will never know the answer to that question. I also never did get to see that chaotic, unruly anarchic mob with their flagrant disregard for the rules, otherwise known as The Humpff Family. But, I think I might have met their Australian cousins!

... AND WE'RE CLIMBING THE STAIRWAY TO...

We made our decision quickly. There was no way we could stay in the stalls for a moment longer, so we made our way to the stairs and started climbing. The Greatest Rock 'n' Roll Band in the World became a muffled sound that could have been anything. We wanted to miss as little as possible, but the events of the evening were taking their toll. The stairs seemed to go on forever and the muffled noise was replaced by muffled cheers, and then a new muffled noise began. How much were we going to miss?

The bare bricks on the walls of the staircase were like a hallucinogenic prison from which there was no escape. We were missing The Greatest Rock 'n' Roll Band in the World and it was our own fault. If we had just gone to our seats we would have seen the lot. We wouldn't be in this strength-sapping race to the sky. We were struggling physically and, just as we thought we were there, we encountered another flight of stairs, and then another. We were scrambling for the gods and the gods were proving to be elusive.

The bare bricks went flashing past, the muffled sound of The Greatest Rock 'n' Roll Band in the World permeated through from the auditorium, and the alcohol dimmed our senses and slowed any progress we made. Eventually we reached the top. Whining, wheezing we burst through the doors and headed towards our seats. The gods were not full. Had some people gone home early? Had some people from the gods been lucky enough to find a corner in the stalls where they could hide? Could it be that *The Concert* hadn't sold out? None of these seemed plausible but it didn't matter because, at last, we had found our own seats. There was room to breathe, and boy did we need to breathe. There was room to dance, but we didn't have the energy to dance. There was room to enjoy what was left of The Greatest Rock 'n' Roll Band in the World.

The sound wasn't so good up in the gods. The Stones songs are so recognisable that we knew what was being sung, but it didn't seem the same any more. We had been so close. We had been on the verge of meeting Mick and Keef. Now, here we were, banished as far away from them as possible. Punished for our naughtiness perhaps.

The punishment didn't stop there. The hippy with the greasy, lank, shoulder length hair was droning.

'The Greatest Rock 'n' Roll Band in the World', he drawled.

'The Greatest Rock 'n' Roll Band in the World', he slurred.

I don't know who he was or what he had taken but he was gone.

'The Greatest Rock 'n' Roll Band in the World.'

'The Greatest Rock 'n' Roll Band in the World.'

'The Greatest Rock 'n' Roll Band in the World.'

'The Greatest Rock 'n' Roll Band in the World.'

'The Greatest Rock 'n' Roll Band in the World.'

He went on and on and on. As The Stones sang, he went on.

'The Greatest Rock 'n' Roll Band in the World.'

If Jagger spoke, he went on.

'The Greatest Rock 'n' Roll Band in the World.'

When the show finished, he went on.

'The Greatest Rock 'n' Roll Band in the World.'

His needle was stuck in a groove and someone needed to dunt the record player but, if anyone had, he would have fallen over.

'The Greatest Rock 'n' Roll Band in the World.'

The Stones left the stage and the noise they had made throughout the night still echoed through The Apollo. The roars and cheers eventually subsided and people reluctantly headed for the exits.

'The Greatest Rock 'n' Roll Band in the World.'

He had no idea where he was.

We, along with almost everyone else, prepared to leave the gods. The usual post-gig hubbub was all around. This had been a special night for everyone.

'The Greatest Rock 'n' Roll Band in the World.'

Still he went on…

'The Greatest Rock 'n' Roll Band in the World'

'The Greatest Rock 'n' Roll Band in the World.'

'The Greatest Rock 'n' Roll Band in the World.'

'The Greatest Rock 'n' Roll Band in the World.'

'The Greatest Rock 'n' Roll Band in the World.'

He may have still been there when they demolished The Apollo.

***

I had lost The Shugmeister. I was on my own. I needed to get to the bus station to catch the last bus and avoid the Boundary Charge. Maybe I could get to The King Burger (yes, King Burger) en route. Did I have time?

Black-pudding supper in hand I gasped my way to the station and climbed on board just before the bus left.

The Shugmeister was already on. The night had reached an end. The memories would live forever but the night was over. Now it was time to come back down to earth. The events of the evening flashed past along with The Royal Infirmary, Alexandra Park and Hogganfield Loch. I had only made the reverse trip about four or five hours ago. How could so many things have happened in such a short space of time?

I arrived home, ready to launch into an account of the evening but then I saw my dad's suit and black tie. Big John's funeral would be taking place the very next morning. Some things are even more important than The Greatest Rock 'n' Roll Band in the World.

20.45 GRCH

Hedonism can only be sustained for so long. There will be exceptions but, for most of us, fighting our way to a bar to buy two pints of lager to hold, while standing watching a band, applauding with our feet and shouting 'Yahoo', gives way to a need for comfort. Lally's Palais was an idea hatched by Glasgow City Council in the run-up to 1990, the year that Glasgow was designated European City of Culture. A few years out from 1990 the idea of Glasgow being cultural was laughable to many and the proposal to spend huge sums of money on a new concert hall seemed fanciful and out of step with 'the way we do things'. The project proceeded nonetheless, with the city's Lord Provost, Pat Lally, taking most of the flak. Like most public building projects, it polarised opinion but, while all this was going on, the bricks were being laid and Glasgow International Concert Hall was built, becoming Glasgow Royal Concert Hall later in the year.

I was aware of the strength of feeling that The Concert Hall generated in the city but mostly allowed this to pass me by and focused on my love of music and radio. The two things go hand in hand and we had reached a point where lines were becoming blurred, with samples being melded onto dance tracks while DJs scratched and mixed and set the foundations of DJs themselves becoming pop stars. Radio fascinated me. Radio is to TV what books are to films. You need imagination to enjoy radio and books. Someone else's imagination makes the decisions on your behalf on TV and in films. Radio had gone through the beginnings of its revolution with commercial players challenging the established BBC output. Radio Clyde had been around since the last day of 1973 and reinvention was always needed to hold the audience's attention.

The Americanisation of radio has always seduced British audiences. From Emperor Roscoe and Paul Gambaccini through to Mr Superbad and the Eye in the Sky. It never seemed quite so glamourous when they read out requests from Sadie in Mount Florida, or updated us on the morning's congestion on Pollokshaws Road, but still we can't get enough of feeling like Americans. Why else did we have a Grand Ole Oprey on Paisley Road West? Why were our nightspots named after American states or cutting-edge New York discos? Why the hell can't we live in a country with time zones?

It's the time zones that mark American radio as special. If you can follow up a time check with 'Eastern Central Time' it is always going to sound better than Richard Park trying to say ten past one in as many different ways as possible.

'It's 10 past one on Radio Clyde. One-ten. Thirteen-ten if you prefer, and here's The Amber Gambler, Billy Ocean, with *Red Light Spells Danger* on Radio Clyde with 50 minutes to go before 2 o'clock.'

Oh, what Richard would have given if he could have said GMT or BST after his time checks, but it would have sounded daft, and Richard would never have wanted to sound daft. Richard wanted to drive across the Brooklyn Bridge, on a sunny Saturday, amid the bumper-to-bumper traffic, but had to make do with The Kincardine Bridge, on a wet Wednesday, to meet up with Derek Johnstone or Davie Provan at East End Park. Richard wanted to be in the city that rocks, the city that never sleeps, but ended up in Glasgow. Richard eventually fled the scene to become a bigwig in The Big Smoke. That's 'Big Smoke', not 'Big Apple', just to be clear.

***

If Richard had hung around for long enough he would have found that Glasgow does have its very own time zone after all. It's known as GRCH and there is only one time of the day when it occurs – 20.45.

When Pat Lally's vision came to fruition I expected the Royal Scottish National Orchestra, Dame Kiri Te Kanawa and Peter Morrison to monopolise this space. The acoustics were much trumpeted and I couldn't see how this would lend itself to bands with dirt under their finger nails. That lot would continue playing their tawdry little dives while Iain Anderson introduced arias, movements and fiddlers' rallies to the residents of Kelvinside and Bearsden. If only I had known.

Jools Holland's Rhythm and Blues Orchestra, Nanci Griffith, Mary Chapin Carpenter, Alison Krauss, Kathy Mattea... and the list goes on. They may not be hardcore rockers but The Concert Hall showed them off at their finest. Soft, sumptuous carpeting. Comfortable seats. Perfect sound system. This was a place which allowed artists to shine and captured those subtle, poignant moments that are often lost among howling feedback, elongated endings and rapturous screaming and cheering. A new chapter had been written. As usual, I was a bit late coming to the party. I hadn't expected to find anything I wanted within those walls but, by the time

I finally pushed those ridiculously large doors open for the first time, I felt this was now the only place I ever wanted to see anyone play. Large crowd, intimate setting. A juxtaposition that seemed to work. Talent could be seen by many and still communicate the tiny nuances that matter.

A typical gig would start with the support act. Well, a typical gig would start with a trip to the bar, to meet up with friends and order the interval drinks… usually soft… further reflecting the ageing process. This always seemed like a very civilised process, but it did mean that things had to run to time so, with the audience seated by about 19.45, the support act could begin.

Now that I think about it, there was another precursor to every GRCH gig. Getting home from work and back out the door in time to get to The Concert Hall was a challenge which normally involved a breakneck drive down the M8 and some speedy parking in Concert Square. Once the car was parked, maybe with just a few minutes to spare, we could begin to relax, while still moving at a fast pace so that we could get on with our night.

'Spare any change, sir?'

It didn't matter how many times I went, I always forgot he would be there.

'Spare any change, sir?'

Of course I could spare some change, but I never did. I didn't have time to spare any change, even if it made me feel guilty. I had friends to meet and interval drinks to order.

'No problem, sir. Thanks for listening, sir.'

When did they change? I grew up being accosted by mad, raving, hairy, flea-ridden, aggressive vagrants in Sauchiehall Street. They always wore filthy, heavy coats and pressed their face up against yours.

'Geez 50 pence for a cuppa tea.'

They didn't ask, they demanded. I would avert my eyes and perform a body swerve, filled with fear for my safety and my record money.

'Ah, f**k you then!'

That's what I expected from vagrants. My dad told me there was a law against vagrancy. These people were supposed to be undesirable, dangerous, deranged… but not any more.

'Have a nice evening, sir. Have a nice evening, madam.'

The vagrancy marketing department must have rebranded the profession in the intervening 25 years and now, as I hurried to cross the road, the guilt was kicking in.

'Enjoy your concert, sir. Enjoy your concert, madam.'

The bleep, bleep, bleep of the green man started to drown him out and his voice tailed off as he turned to the next concert goer.

'Spare any change, sir?'

'No problem. Thanks for listening, sir.'

'Have a nice evening, sir.'

'Enjoy your concert, sir.'

With hands shaken, hugs exchanged and interval drinks ordered we could shuffle into our seats to soak up the support act. The great unknown. Hit or miss. Who knows?

'Paul who?'

'Thorn, I think. Never heard of him.'

Paul Thorn supported Jools Holland and his Rhythm and Blues Orchestra. Jools is a safe pair of hands when it comes to the acts he introduces so we hoped high, but had no expectations.

Paul Thorn was a storyteller. He could rock it up but the magic was in the stories, the backdrop to the songs, the words to the songs themselves. Anyone who says he had an 800lb Jesus in his garden is staking quite a claim. Writing a song about it moves things on to another level. Buying a flock of ceramic sheep, to keep the 800lb Jesus company, moves the story from the realms of fantasy into something that is so ridiculous it has to be true.

Paul Thorn ran the full gamut of emotions that night. Songs celebrating the joy of love and others bearing the soul and the tortures of breaking up. Songs that made us laugh and cry. Even a song about his friend who was a stripper and whose daddy was a preacher. Daddy had no idea what she did when she went out in the evenings but Paul Thorn enlightened us. He also distracted us from our interval drinks as his CD was a must-buy. The fact that we bought it from him personally made it feel special. Incidentally, if the last few paragraphs encourage you to buy Paul Thorn's 'Hammer & Nail' CD (does anyone do that any more?), let it run after you think it has finished. It will be worth it.

Only Jools Holland could follow that and still bring the house down.

The age-old dilemma of following a superb support act has haunted the top stars since the dawn of time. Stories of Bruce Forsyth berating opening stand-ups for being too good still circulate in showbiz circles. The terror of being upstaged can destabilise competent performers and skew reviews in such a way that they are portrayed in a bad light, which can have devastating effects on their careers. Quite why Alison Krauss thought it was a good idea to have Carrie Newcomer as support puzzled me. A high-risk strategy if ever there was one.

I had never heard of Carrie Newcomer before that night. Her name tickled me a bit because, to me, she was a bit of a newcomer and it took me back to *The Green Citizen* and *The Pink Times* and how they called unknown footballers A N Other, and if there was a 'Newman' in the team I was left pondering whether this was his real name or maybe just someone the journalists didn't know.

Carrie Newcomer was a storyteller too. A singer-songwriter who could say, in a few words, what most of us would struggle to say in a lifetime. She didn't have an 800lb Jesus to boast about but she made simple things sound extraordinary. She sang about the junk she kept in her attic, and we can all relate to that, but her junk wasn't useless. Her junk was a lifetime of memories, a lifetime of stories. Thankfully, Carrie Newcomer made sure those memories were not forgotten. She sang about her daughter Amelia. She loved her daughter, as you would expect, but the intricacies and nuances of what she loved most about her was what made the tears come to the eyes. She sang of endless hours sitting in a fishing boat with her father. The youngest of three girls, she became his de facto son to replace the one he never had. There is nothing remarkable about sitting in a fishing boat but the GRCH audience seemed to transport themselves there, with her and her father, respecting the silence for fear of scaring the fish away. When she finished, you could have heard a plastic plectrum drop, as the sound of the last guitar string drifted away downstream before a torrent of applause erupted and tore through the room.

Somewhere, behind the stage, Alison Krauss sat, presumably shaking, as the clock ticked closer to 20.45 GRCH.

Once the interval drinks had been consumed and the last bell had rung it was time to take our seats in the main auditorium. This is when the sensation would begin. Excitement, anticipation, call it what you will. At 20.45 GRCH there was something in the air. This was what we had come to see. This was what the effort was all about. Rushing home from work, bombing down the M8, running the gauntlet of polite vagrants, shaking hands, hugging, ordering interval drinks, watching the support act, debriefing the support act, listening for the bell and filing into our seats. Somehow, the frenetic nature of everything that had brought us here would evaporate to be replaced by a sensation so enticing that it would only be possible to experience it at one time, in one place. It was 20.45 GRCH.

As I looked down from my side view, just above the stage, I saw Mr Personality, Jools Holland emerge from beneath me. A wave, a nod, a wink, a smile. The Rhythm and Blues Orchestra were in full swing and Jools took up his place at the piano and we were off and running.

As I looked down from upstairs, my view straight onto the stage this time, I saw Mary Chapin Carpenter walk on, wave, say 'Hi', count to four and off she went.

As I looked from my prime central seat downstairs, I saw Alison Krauss take to the stage with her band Union Station. I felt for her. At least she had come team handed. Her version of *Now That I've Found You* had cut through and, thanks to that, a whole new audience had opened up and had come to see her brand of country. It was country, wasn't it?

The new material had suggested a crossover into the mainstream. Soon, pariahs like Ronan Keating would be passing her songs off as his own. If you care about music, even after all these years, please don't let that happen. But I digress, the night had turned. The GRCH audience were always an appreciative bunch but the buzz at the interval had all been about Carrie Newcomer. It was about who we had seen, not who we were about to see. Most people felt the same as me, totally blown away. I would never have believed it until that moment but now there was a connection between Alison Krauss and Bruce Forsyth.

Union Station got things going and Alison sang as only Alison can. The memory of Carrie Newcomer was still lingering in the auditorium but, bit by bit, we were being brought round. Alison's vocal abilities were unsurpassed. Everything we heard on record was real. No technical enhancement needed here thank you. Alison even took the time to thank Carrie Newcomer. For what? For completely upstaging her? The evening rolled along. These guys new what they were doing. Alison produced a fiddle and we were in Bluegrass country. The pace of the evening was now breakneck and we were treated not just to a fabulous singer with a band, but to a band who were very much worthy of their equal billing. *When You Say Nothing At All* brought the house down and the gig ended with Bluegrass fiddles trading licks and, needless to say, rapturous applause from the GRCH crowd.

Alison Krauss was never troubled by Carrie Newcomer's presence as support. Whether you call it folk, country, traditional or whatever, the word 'support' has a different meaning in that world. Having a support act is not about making up the numbers or warming up the audience. It's about introducing someone new to the world, giving someone a break, providing *support* to a fellow performer. Alison Krauss had grafted and learned. One day, in the past, someone would have given her a break. That someone didn't fear her, they just wanted people to hear her. That someone was sure enough of their own ability just as Alison Krauss was of her own. Thank God for Alison Krauss, and all the others who are willing to bring new talent through for our benefit, not for theirs.

None of which really explains the whipping incident which took place upstairs on the evening that Al Green came to town.

Al Green. That's all you need to say. Maybe stick 'Reverend' in front but Al Green is Al Green. 'Nuff said.

I didn't need any encouragement to go see Al Green but Lonesome Dave added a note of intrigue in the run-up to the gig. Al Green was fairly new to his 'Reverend' status and the previous year Lonesome Dave had travelled to London to see the great man. While enjoying a pre-show drink, Dave was earywigging on the conversations taking place around him. In his left ear, he could hear two girls discussing Deuteronomy, Chapter 5. In his right ear, another two girls were discussing the new album by Prince. Which incarnation of The Reverend Al Green would dominate this gig remained a bit of a mystery.

I did the usual Schumacher down the M8, bodyswerved the frightfully lovely vagrants, ordered the interval drinks and we took our seats upstairs. Our seats were like those ones you might have sat in if you have ever been to The City Halls to see something classical. A side view that comes with a guaranteed crick in the neck by the end of the night. I just didn't expect the whipping.

The couple beside us were quite young. I was intrigued about what brought them to see Al Green. Judging by the overwhelming smell of alcohol and the obvious drunkenness I am guessing it wasn't Al's Reverend status, but I could be wrong. There were lots of jerky movements, standing up, sitting down, cuddling, kissing, fondling. I hoped they weren't going to keep that up all the way through. At least they were on my left and the stage was to my right. I could just ignore them. That would be the best strategy.

I want to say that the support act was John Martyn's Blues Band, but I can't be sure and claim mitigating circumstances on this occasion. The first thrash took me completely by surprise and left me dazed and disorientated.

I had no idea where it came from. The second one came quickly after. Then a third and a fourth. It was the young female to my left. She may have been drunk but it was definitely her dishing out the lashes. She was attractive, from what I could see of her through the pain. She had long hair with crinkly curls. She was oblivious to my suffering.

Another thrash came along, then another and another. Each one lacerated the side of my face. It was her hair that was to blame. The long, crinkly curls. She had an affectation, possibly enhanced by drink or maybe just a life trait. She unconsciously, and involuntarily, flicked her head from side to side on a regular basis causing her hair to flow, violently, from right to left and back again. If I was being thrashed on my left cheek, her partner would be getting it on the right. Maybe he liked it. I didn't! I was struggling to enjoy my night out and she was too uncaring, or drunk, to bother.

The interval came and they went off to the bar. By 20.45 GRCH they were nowhere to be seen. On one level, this was an act of heresy. Al Green was about to come on stage and their seats were empty.

'Father, forgive them.; for they know not what they do.'

Luke23:34

On another level, this was an act of mercy, a reward for my patience. Al Green was about to come on stage and I would be able to enjoy the spectacle.

'To one who strikes you in the cheek, offer the other one also… and as you wish that others would do to you, do so to them.'

Luke 6:29-31

But it was too good to be true. Somewhere during the second verse of *How Can You Mend a Broken Heart* another thunderous thrash rained down on me. They were back, if possible even drunker than before.

Mercifully, the thirst for drink, or passion or both took over and they disappeared, pawing at one another, with him muttering lewd suggestions to her as they unsteadily negotiated the stairs to the exit. I think he said something about her 'big ass' and 'working on that zipper'. You know, the kind of thing Prince might have said.

I was able to enjoy the rest of the night. Al Green, resplendent in white suit, made his way among his congregation and distributed red roses, mostly to the ladies, and bounced up and down on the balls of his feet as his falsetto filled the room and filled us with the joy of his spirit. Al Green – a true star, a true icon, a true legend.

KETTLE CONNECTIONS

The GRCH has an upstairs, as we have already established, but it would be remiss not to mention the other upstairs part – the Strathclyde Suite. It would also be wrong not to mention the crowning glory of GRCH – Celtic Connections.

The festival now stretches far and wide across the city but the hub has always been The Concert Hall. If you brand your festival as Celtic Connections you open up a world of potential where audiences can trace a line from the sounds of the traditional Scottish folk music that we grew up with, through journeys to far flung places where musical fusion has taken place time and again and our influences infiltrate theirs, and theirs infiltrate ours and the world becomes a richer place because of it. In its loosest sense, branding yourself as Celtic Connections also allows you to have Tom Jones playing in the main auditorium, but the hidden gems are often to be found upstairs, and upstairs again.

The beauty of Celtic Connections is that you can take a chance on any show and it is unlikely you will come away disappointed. If nothing else, you will be impressed by the showmanship and finely honed craft of the performers. There are times when you will feel uneasy after hearing Tommy Sands sing of a tit-for-tat sectarian killing, or Karine Polwart sing, in Scots tongue, of ethnic cleansing atrocities in Srebrenica. And there are times when you will simply be taken by the most pleasant surprises you could ever imagine.

This particular Saturday night promised nothing. There were three acts on the bill and we hadn't heard of any of them. The Strathclyde Suite was set up in cabaret style with tables and chairs dotted around the floor rather than in the more familiar rows. Despite the lack of big names there was a good turn out and it was tricky to move around, order drinks and negotiate you way back to your table. The first act came and went. Good, steady start. Nothing to complain about there. The second act came on, The French Alligators. Virtually no one in the room had heard of them. We read about them in the programme. They were from New Orleans. That gave us a clue about what to expect. Something Cajun.

The French Alligators took to the stage and reeled off a couple of numbers to loosen themselves off. Nothing remarkable. The leader of the band was wearing a tatty hat which, along with his farmhand garments, made him look a bit daft.

'Look, it's The Village Idiot', I heard someone beside me say.

The leader addressed the audience. He wasn't going to shake off The Village Idiot tag easily. He spoke in broken English and, although trying to be friendly, seemed to be generally incompetent.

Another number was struck up and his tiny accordion squeezed out something from back home as he smiled, and maybe leered, at those closest to the front. On either side of him, women began to dance. Their dresses seemed just as shambolic as their leader's garb but they danced, and the band played and the audience warmed to this strange and heady mixture from a place far, far away.

The leader spoke again. To my side, I heard another 'village idiot' comment. The leader spoke on and, as he did, the audience loosened and laughter ensued. No one knew yet whether they were laughing with or at him but he was cutting through and even the guy who kept shouting 'village idiot' was only doing it through laughter and tears.

The French Alligators had been toying with us. They ripped into another tune and the musicianship cranked up several levels. The dancers started to show off their moves. The tiny Cajun accordion sprang into feverish life and the Strathclyde Suite audience gave way and allowed itself to be transported down the Mississippi on the Steamboat Natchez, stopping off at all the little night spots on the way and learning the history of that wonderful part of the world. The Village Idiot and one of his dancers performed one of the most intricate routines I have ever seen. I doubt that Scottish Ballet have ever taken on anything so complex and this would go far beyond the abilities of the average *Strictly* professional. They seemed certain to become entangled on so many occasions, such were the complexities of the piece but, on each occasion, they emerged unscathed, with looks of fake surprise on their faces, as if they had solved one of those impossible Christmas cracker puzzles.

The French Alligators left an indelible mark on Glasgow and on me, too, so much so that I have no memory of who was top of the bill that night. For me, and I suspect for everyone else present, the star of the show was The Village Idiot and he would be welcome back anytime.

The intimacy of the Strathclyde Suite lends itself to certain performances. The obvious conclusion to jump to is that this is where new talent is blooded – acts who don't yet have enough of a following to fill bigger venues or maybe acts who are big in their part of the world but little known locally. That, however, is not always the case and sometimes the Strathclyde Suite can be just the right place to try something new, even if you could fill the room downstairs in your own right.

Mary Coughlan is one such act. Irish, not to be messed with, filthy sense of humour, troubled past. The perfect ingredients for someone who sings songs with meaning. Mary Coughlan has a jazz background but to pigeonhole her would be to do her a disservice. Mary Coughlan has a substantial following but here she was, just her and a pianist, on stage in the Strathclyde Suite on a weeknight, trying out a few things and grumbling about how a cancelled ferry meant she had to travel that afternoon and it had all been a bit touch and go time wise. Not that you would have noticed.

We did get some jazz as Billie Holiday's music was a big part of what Mary Coughlan was doing at the time but she sings powerful songs from closer to home, too, and her expose of the horrors of the Magdalene Laundries cannot help but make listeners sit up and pay attention. She's an entertainer first and foremost, though, and there was humour in every link and something comical about this force of nature transporting us to a Berlin nightclub of the 1930s to purr, in her smoky tones, *I Want To Be Seduced*.

Eddi Reader is another who could fill the main auditorium comfortably but seems to move around the circuit in whichever direction she chooses. Aly Bain and Phil Cunningham are seldom far away, but I saw Eddi as part of a kind of supergroup in the Strathclyde Suite. You know the type of thing, John McCusker and all his mates. It's an opportunity to work together, to try out some new things, to introduce some new singers, to entertain the crowd. That'll do for me thank you very much.

I knew Eddi Reader was talented and I knew that she loved her music. I even knew that she was versatile but she surpassed herself here. Just before the gig, or maybe even during it, someone thought it would be a good idea to end with the Nina Simone classic *Feelin' Good*. Eddi was familiar with the song but didn't know the words. Someone handed her a piece of paper and she ran through it backstage during the interval. I only know this because she told the audience. She decided to go for it and thank goodness she did. She made it her own. The power in her voice distracted us from the fact that she held the paper in her hand all the way through. Slick doesn't begin to describe it. Her eyes closed, her arms outstretched, her garments flowing in the lights. Perfect.

***

There is something tawdry about staring at a venue in its naked, daytime state. The magic of the evening creates the ambience, the feeling, the setting that we need for our enjoyment. The harsh reality of the day brings the smell of stale booze, the beer barrels, the basic, unimaginative black walls and curtains. My own brush with behind the scenes at The Apollo in the hope of meeting Mick and Keef had taught me that there was a time to see the places we cherished and there were other times when we should not look. It seemed strange, therefore, that I was looking forward to being in the Strathclyde Suite, before 10am, subjecting myself to pressure that should have ended 20 years before.

The original idea had been to study for a professional qualification. It didn't happen, but it irked me and eventually the itch needed to be scratched. The plan was to sit 14 papers in the shortest time possible, which was about two years.

I embarked on this at 38 and the target was to qualify by 40. When I heard that the exams would be in the Strathclyde Suite, I felt strangely reassured. This was a place in which I'd had so many enjoyable moments. This would be different, of course, but, other than sitting the exams in my own living room, this felt like the next best thing.

When I arrived for the first exam it felt wrong that signs saying 'Silence' and 'Quiet please' were dotted around the walls. This was a room that normally resounded with life and sound, with characters, with stories, with laughter, with applause... never with silence.

The silence was observed impeccably by the students sitting in neat and tidy rows in this oasis of calm, tucked away from the hubbub of Sauchiehall Street and any potentially offending roadworks. It was 10 o'clock in the morning. There would be no noise from the main auditorium. Even the rows of tables and the sense of order demanded by the invigilators, which seemed far removed from the creativity and artistry that was normally on display, felt normal, calm and serene.

Exams came and went, twice a year, June and December. Each time, the Strathclyde Suite sat silent, readying itself for what was to come that weekend, later that month, later that year, but still maintaining that respectful atmosphere in which grades would be earned and career paths decided.

The final three exams came along, one day after another. The first passed off without incident but the following day some noise was heard. Some building work must have been going on inside The Concert Hall. The acoustic design of the building deadened some of the sound but drilling noises could be heard and vibrations could be felt. We didn't need this! We had come so far. Would it be too much just to let us finish our exams in silence, the way it's meant to be?

The drilling finished and so did the exam. Slightly shaken, we left the building; hopefully not too much damage had been done to our hopes.

I think we were about halfway through the final exam when we heard a new noise. It was distant, but there was something. Never mind, where was I? Oh yes, that was it, the net present value of the investment based on an inherent rate of return of... There it was again. But what was it? Distant shouting? I tried to block it out, to keep calm and carry on.

... net present value... rate of return... project term eight years... initial investment...

Oh bugger! There it was again. Seeping through the walls. Getting louder. Sounded like kids. Why would that be? Guided tour? Maybe that was it. Should be over soon. I tried to focus.

... initial investment £2million... what was the term again? I'd lost my train of thought. AARGH! I had to read it all again.

The noise intensified. These kids weren't going anywhere. Someone was egging them on. They must have been on the other side of the wall, or maybe a little further away – maybe in the main auditorium. Why would that be?

They were shouting about spouts, handles and lids!

What the...?

'WHAT'S INSIDE THE SINGING KETTLE?'

How could they allow this to happen? I was on the brink of passing my final exams but was being sabotaged by 1,000 kids who had come to see The Singing Kettle! Someone had to be accountable for this. These exams were serious. What did they think it was? Christmas?

It was, actually. It was the middle of December and panto season had begun. Some of us had our heads wedged so far inside our textbooks that we had forgotten that people were allowed to enjoy themselves. The Singing Kettle wasn't a pantomime, as such. It was a phenomenon. My own kids hadn't put in an appearance by that time so I never got to see the show, but I heard it. Boy did I hear it.

IN LIFE, IN DEATH,
OH LORD, ABIDE WITH ME

I had booked the day off work. Just as well. I felt queasy, and uneasy. I was reliving the previous night. How could we be so naïve to think that we could just march up and *meet* Mick and Keef? We had *seen* The Stones though. A lifetime ambition fulfilled at 20. The Greatest Rock 'n' Roll Band in the World. Oh, I had forgotten about him. I wondered if he was still there, still muttering.

My head was sore. The aftermath of the black-pudding supper was causing my stomach some discomfort. I didn't know the final result from the FA Cup Final replay. Tottenham were winning when I last looked. When was that? Half-time? Probably later. I remembered going back to The Ivanhoe. Why did we go back to The Ivanhoe? Something to do with the bouncers... and vodka. The very thought turned my stomach. Could the FA Cup Final have gone to extra-time?

My thoughts were interrupted when I saw my own suit and black tie. Big John's funeral was at 10 o'clock. Why did I say I would go? If I didn't, maybe I wouldn't be missed. But it was Big John. I thought about all the good things he did, all the good things his family did, and all they ever got passed downstairs in return was the thumping noise of football in the hall, the irritating kerrang of golf balls hitting the tin bucket and a couple of Gilbert O'Sullivan jumpers for Karen.

My mum was a great knitter. People came from here, there and everywhere to ask her to knit jumpers, cardigans, baby bootees and pram covers. If they paid for the wool, she did the hard graft. She liked to experiment and, when Gilbert O'Sullivan discarded his flat cap and short trousers and started wearing jumpers with a great bit 'G' on the front, she wanted to get in on the act. I was still of an age when the idea of owning a Gilbert O'Sullivan jumper with a tastefully sized 'K' on the front was exciting so she worked out her own pattern and, before I knew it, I was the envy of the school with my navy blue jumper with two light-blue hoops on each sleeve, another two around the chest and with a nice gap at the front to accommodate the 'K'. I was the class celebrity. You could buy Gilbert O'Sullivan jumpers in the shops but mine was unique. No one, anywhere, had their very own bespoke version. Only me.

The brown-with-fawn version followed, meaning I could wear a Gilbert O'Sullivan jumper pretty much every day if I chose. What I didn't know was that someone, somewhere, regarded my jumpers with envious eyes: Big John's daughter Karen to be precise. One year my junior, she knew that I would grow out of them eventually and slowly but surely put herself first in the queue for the hand-me-downs.

I had to have a bath, and some breakfast. You can't be late for a funeral. But I felt awful. This wasn't going to be easy but it had to be done. I dragged myself to Daldowie Crematorium and sat, looking across at Big John's family. I remembered the feeling of delight when I came home from school to a locked door and knocked on Big John's instead. Tea, cakes, Kit Kats, Tunnock's Carmel Wafers.

'Eat up, you're in your Auntie Isa's.'

Today wasn't the day for that. Today was a sad day. A day when a family said goodbye. A friendly, loving, caring family who deserved more time with their husband, their dad.

Abide With Me started and snapped me out of my thoughts for the family and started off some others. The FA Cup Final crowd came together to sing this hymn of hope before kick-off and I was there, at Wembley, through the lens of a TV screen in a Buchanan Street pub. Then I was on a terracing, a large, high-sloping terracing with green barriers for people to rest on. I was too small to reach the barriers, so I picked up ring pulls from beer cans. As I did so, Rangers crashed in goal after goal. They finished with six, Aberdeen only got one. Rangers were in the cup final. I had a ring pull from a beer can for every goal that was scored that day, but the thought of beer brought me back to The Ivanhoe and The Apollo and The Smirnoff Ambush and my stomach lurched, and my head throbbed, and *Abide With Me* ended and I could hear sobbing and realised that my discomfort would end soon. For others, it would take more time.

We said our last goodbye to Big John and, on our way home, my dad, bizarrely, decided to go to Reid Bros TV shop in Dennistoun to buy a colour TV. The first images we saw on it were of Pope John Paul ll arriving in the UK. The following day we saw England's Paul Mariner break Scottish hearts with a header, the only goal of the game, at Hampden.

I didn't need a colour TV to see life in all its glory. I also didn't know that one day I would marvel at Dean Owens of The Felsons seamlessly medley from Bruce Springsteen's *I'm on Fire* into Blondie's *Heart of Glass* in a tent on Glasgow Green. I didn't know that The Five Blind Boys of

Alabama would raise the roof at The Pavilion on a sunny May Bank Holiday Monday, making us all see the light, literally, as the gig finished before 7pm. I didn't know there would be a place we would call The Armadillo to which The Mavericks and Van Morrison would come calling for my pleasure, as would Wee Jimmy Krankie for my kids. I didn't know that I would see some of the finest comics of their generation – Ben Elton, Lenny Henry, Harry Enfield and Who Dares Wins, to name but a few, and I didn't know that I would see The Nutcracker or La Fille Mal Garde or Prokofiev's Romeo and Juliet or Sing-A-Long-A Sound Of Music at The Theatre Royal.

The line that joins the dots between Slade at The Apollo and *A Midsummer Night's Dream* at The GRCH is a jaggy one. There was the occasional trough, but mostly there were peaks. Some performers, and some venues, have gone without mention: Beth Neilson Chapman, loaded with the cold, fingerless mittens on hands, battling on like a true pro in a freezing cold Fruitmarket; the hardy perennials who stayed up into the small hours in places like The Central Hotel to satisfy the unquenchable thirst of the Celtic Connections diehards; the young, aspiring hopefuls who put on their own gig at The Ramshorn Theatre only to see two overdressed, overage, out-of-place characters turn up to witness a young girl from Ayrshire take to the stage and tell her friend in the front row that she was 'brickin' it' before killing us softly with her song. Many people have helped my jaggy line to be drawn. More on that later.

Before that, I feel the need to say a few words on the Boundary Charge, which put the fear of God into me and many others. If you have ever sat in a taxi, stuck at a set of lights, watching the meter tick inexorably up and up, imagine how it feels when you know that 20% will be added to the number you see. In my experience, it was better to jump out at the boundary and walk the rest of the way. For me, that was 10 minutes. For others, it could be much longer.

That's one of the reasons I have stuck rigidly within the city boundary so far – an inbuilt fear of the cost of leaving. But there were many other gigs, and it would be a shame not to mention some of them. The question is, are *you* prepared to cross the boundary?

BEYOND THE BOUNDARY

SALT AND WHAT?

For the benefit of real Glaswegians I won't go through the agony of explaining what the title of this chapter refers to. They already know. Suffice to say, we will start and end with a fish supper.

I followed my instructions to the letter. They had been given to me by a member of the constabulary, after all. Blue bus into town, corporation bus to Scotstoun. It feels like we've been here before, doesn't it? Well, that's where you're wrong. At this point in my life I still didn't know that railway arches were a thing. All I knew was that I had to be in Scotstoun around four-ish where I would meet up with my old school pal who was now simply known as The Polis.

We had gone through secondary school joined at the hip, but a lucrative move to a West End town house beckoned and The Polis became a bit more inaccessible as a result. Our meetings were few and far between, but we still had one thing in common. Queen!

The Polis was ahead of me on this. He saw Queen at The Glasgow Apollo in 1979. I was insanely jealous. Now, about a year later, we were heading off east into a world of the unknown.

We decided it would be a good idea to get a fish supper before we left and ate it in his car. The wonderful aroma of fish, chips, batter, salt and vinegar lingered all along the M8 as we speculated about what was in store.

I had heard all about *Death on Two Legs* more times than I cared to remember. The Polis often talked about that night at The Apollo and how those haunting, distant piano keys emerged from the darkness, only to be overtaken by sinister electric guitar sounds which screeched to a halt and were replaced with a piano, this time sedate but only for seconds before the band's inimitable signature sound emerged and Freddie savaged the management company that had cheated them out of the rewards they so richly deserved.

Every time he relayed this to me I just felt waves of jealously. Why hadn't I gone along? Can't remember. Too late now.

The Polis explained that this was how Queen had opened their Apollo show. I could picture it. Blindsiding the audience, just like The Commodores. Different sound, same idea. If only I had been there.

My time had come. The Polis drove and I spectated as we mused over the opening of this new show that Queen were bringing to towns up and down the UK, but seemingly not mine. Bizarrely, The Polis believed that Queen would start their show with *Death on Two Legs*. He figured that the auditorium would be in darkness and the audience would hear distant, haunting piano keys, which would be overtaken by sinister electric guitar sounds which, in turn, would screech to a halt, to be replaced by a few seconds of sedate piano before Queen's inimitable signature sound would emerge and Freddie would savage the management company that cheated them out of the rewards they so richly deserved. I don't think he put it quite like that, but that was the gist.

I wasn't so sure. Bands had albums to sell and gigs were vehicles for doing just that. For me, it had to be *Flash*. The single had been huge and Queen's soundtrack added so much to the film *Flash Gordon*. If you wanted to open a show with a distant sound emerging from the darkness what better than that drilling, bassie sound, making the floor vibrate, taking the brain to the point of delusion before replacing it with the shock of the first *Flash!* Lights were what you needed at that point. Bright, blinding lights. The Polis wasn't convinced.

I tried to reason with him. Did he think that Queen would start every show with *Death on Two Legs*? The band had already had about 20 hits. There was no sign of that stopping. Some songs would have to be sacrificed, no matter how good they were, perhaps with one, very obvious, exception.

There was no shifting him. It would be *Death on Two Legs* and that was that. I was just as bad. It would be *Flash*. Just wait and see. We decided it would be a good idea to roll our windows down a little bit as the lingering smell of fish, chips, batter, salt and vinegar was becoming a little overwhelming.

The journey along the M8 to an Edinburgh gig is a wonderful thing. People make this journey on a solitary basis day in, day out, but when you are going to a gig, you seldom go alone. The stark, barren, dullness that normally accompanies motorway driving is replaced by tingling anticipation, but what's new there? You're going to a gig, after all. Only there is more at stake. If it's a weeknight, you have to head off early. The timing has to be precise. The rush hour traffic needs to subside and you have to leave early enough to get there on time. It's a fine balancing act, not for the fainthearted.

Take the gig at St Giles' Cathedral, for example. The Shugmeister is not known for arriving early for anything but he usually makes it on time, if a little flustered. We knew we were cutting it neat when we set off but didn't really factor in the impact of driving into the city centre and trying to find somewhere to park. We thought we knew our way around the capital but we didn't.

We parked in The St James Centre and followed our noses to The Royal Mile. There is so much history in such a compact space but it was lost on us as we barged our way to the doors of St Giles', tickets in hand, breathless, flustered, late.

The Five Blind Boys of Alabama had knocked our socks off the year before at The Pavilion in Glasgow. To see them in such a setting as St Giles', evangelising and entertaining simultaneously, was too good a chance to pass up. We were ushered in from the foyer, the way you always are in churches, even if this was one of the grandest of them all. The Blind Boys were in full swing but something not quite right. We couldn't find a seat for a start. We lurched forward and crept back. Every forward movement resulted in obscuring someone's view, every retreat spoiled ours. The seats facing the stage had all been taken. In fact, they weren't seats, they were pews. And it wasn't a stage, it was... OK, we may have proceeded through a narthex, a nave and an aisle, and there may have been choir stalls and a transept and who knows what else. The problem was that we couldn't see a thing and the sound wasn't that great either.

We weren't the only ones. Everyone who didn't have a seat had to find a vantage point. We happened to be last to arrive and all the vantage points had gone. The Blind Boys did their stuff and we tried our best to enjoy it, but it didn't hit the heights of The Pavilion show. But don't take that as a slur on the city of Edinburgh or the beautiful Cathedral of St Giles. On another day, I would gladly have whiled away some time, marvelling at the architecture and regaling the pillars as great feats of construction from days long before mechanisation and industrialisation. Pillars say so much in the context of a church. Yes, they hold it up. But to have held one up for centuries takes some doing. And those pillars, and that strength, give hope to many that they, too, can be pillars in their own right. Pillars of the community. Strong, secure, safe, caring, comforting pillars on which The Word can be carried, or that someone in need can lean on. Those pillars worked against us the night we went to see The Blind Boys. But those pillars have more to do than accommodate me and my concert-going needs. Those pillars have bigger fish to fry.

And so we go from one extreme to another. For every frantic dash of The Shugmeister, there is the supreme military planning of Jim The Nipper. You may recall that Jim is a fan of silky soul. I'm quite partial to it myself, but where Jim would happily spend the rest of time in the company of Alexander O'Neal, Luther Vandross, Whitney Houston and all their mates. I need some Otis Redding, Aretha Franklin and James Brown thrown in to introduce some rawness to the genre. Jim, however, is the kind of person you want to have around because he knows about everything before anyone else does. He plans in advance, books in advance, takes control and makes a night of it.

That's probably why I found myself sitting at a table in a restaurant, a good 90 minutes or so before Natalie Cole took to the stage in Livingston. There was no rush, but there was an itinerary. We left early, negotiated the M8 comfortably, drew up outside the appointed eatery and proceeded to have fish and chips in one of those places where the salt and vinegar comes in little sachets whether you like it or not.

Natalie Cole? Talented in her own right or living off the glories of her father? I would say the former. She could sing, she could work a crowd and she could duet with someone who wasn't there. The miracles of technology allowed her to duet with Nat King Cole on *Unforgettable*. No one would bat an eyelid now but at the time it seemed like a nice thing to do. George Benson didn't agree.

Some time later we were at the SECC in Glasgow to see George Benson, a self-confessed Nat King Cole devotee. George didn't fancy this mingling of past with present. He sang his own version of the duet, taking both parts, singing beautifully on the Nat King Cole parts and screeching comically on Natalie's.

***

But I digress. The meter is running and, with every mile we travel, your bill increases exponentially. I seem to remember that The Polis's car was somewhere around Harthill Services, windows slightly open, trying to let a concoction of odours escape, along with an awkward silence over how Queen would open their show.

The gig was at Ingliston, but it wasn't the mega gig of 1982. This one was in one of the big sheds and we seemed to have arrived in tonnes of time. It was standing only and there really wasn't anything to do other than wait. The shed was empty at the time and all I could think of was herds or cows being exhibited at The Royal Highland Show. Was this really a suitable venue for one of rock's most talented superpowers?

Gradually, the shed filled and we claimed a vantage point, not too near the stage, not too far away. The stage seemed to have been plonked there, in a corner. It wasn't even that high. Darkness fell and after what seemed like an eternity sounds emerged, although the overwhelming feature was light. Huge, piercing lasers penetrated the eye sockets as they swung this way and that, rendering the audience momentarily blind one section at a time. As our eyes recovered we tried to glimpse the stage but the light made it impossible to see if there was any activity. The crowd reacted wildly but the whole experience was disorientating and no one really knew what was going on.

A sound started to drift in, but from where? Another sweep of the lasers and my eyes retreated for fear of never working again. The beams seemed to be penetrating my brain. I felt a dull thud, or maybe I heard a dull thud, and then another and another and another. Suddenly the lasers vanished and the stage was alight. Freddie Mercury honed into view and the cowshed was filled with the sound of *Flash!* Oh you beauty!

The Polis just looked at me. It was too loud for words but there was no need for words. I had won that round but that wasn't the point. He would always be one ahead of me because he was at The Apollo in 1979 and I wasn't. Incidentally, I did a bit of research on that gig, just to make sure I got my dates right. Some kind soul had posted a set list. Queen didn't start with *Death on Two Legs* at all. It was number six on the list.

The Polis had a bit of form on that type of thing. I once found him grooving away to himself on the first tee at Lethamhill Golf Couse. As I got nearer, I heard that he was singing along to Jermaine Jackson's *Let's Get Serious*, only he was singing *Mass Hysteria* instead. You never quite knew if he meant it or not. But he was a bigger Queen fan than most and never lost his love for them. Sadly, he's no longer around, but his family kept his sense of madness alive as we left the crematorium to the sounds of *Another One Bites the Dust*. It's what he would have wanted.

***

Lonesome Dave had Edinburgh down to a tee. Thank goodness this is in writing. If a Glaswegian mentions Edinburgh and tea in the same sentence, it can cause offence! Dave's work took him to the capital often and he knew the city streets like the back of his hand. As usual, I just had to turn up and do as I was told and he would do the rest. There was no nonsense about pre-theatre meals. It was all about getting to the gig with minimum fuss and maximum enjoyment.

I've never been much of a Fringe-goer. But Lonesome Dave transported me to a Fringe gig one weeknight in the late 80s. There were four acts on the bill. The first was a band and one of its members was playing a tea chest. It couldn't have been, could it? No, it wasn't. I never did get to see The Humpff Family. Second up, no idea. Third? This was who I came to see. The inimitable Arnold Brown.

Arnold Brown had a lazy, understated, laid-back style of delivery but his gags were razor sharp. He made a great deal of being both Glaswegian and Jewish. No football team to support, apparently. He put forward the case for tearooms. You seldom see a fight outside a tearoom. And, just to be topical, he was helped by the fact that Princess Fergie's first child had just been born. We were going through the 'what will they call her' ritual. Arnold suggested 'parasite'. And why not?

The evening was rounded off with some jazz from Fiona Duncan, and damned good it was too. I really should do something about my Fringe deficiency.

***

The Playhouse, it seemed to me, was to Edinburgh, what The Apollo was to Glasgow. Lonesome Dave dragged me there a few times, most notably to see B.B. King. Of course, we did the classic thing of disappearing off to the bar during the support act. There was a TV screen in the bar, relaying what was happening on stage. That's just as good, isn't it?

No, it's not. It was someone with a big hat who went on to become very famous.

We didn't miss a second of B.B. King, though. I could use the word 'legend'. I could talk about the man loving his guitar so much that he gave her a name. I could mention that he had been thrust into the limelight due to his collaboration with U2 on *When Love Comes to Town*. But B.B. King doesn't need sycophantic oiks like me to talk him up. He went beyond that a long time ago.

Speaking of guitars, how about Ry Cooder? It went something like this. Lonesome Dave was due to go to see Little Village at The Playhouse along with his lovely wife, but she wasn't well. Poor soul. As most people know, one person's loss is another's gain and I was the gainer on that occasion.

I don't want to insult anyone's musical intelligence but just in case you don't know, Little Village was a coming together of four musical aficionados. Drummer Jim Keltner may be referred to, unkindly, as a session musician. A quick peek at his CV and you will see names including Bob Dylan, Roy Orbison, Sheryl Crow, Oasis and almost all of The Beatles. Session musician my arse! John Hiatt did most of the vocals. Our very own Nick Lowe was in there too, being *Cruel to be Kind*, obviously, and Ry Cooder completed the line-up with his mesmerising ability on guitar and the occasional blast of *Little Sister* thrown in for good measure. They had all worked together on Hiatt's album and decided to take their show on the road. I'm so glad they did. Lonesome Dave wouldn't even take the money for the ticket.

***

I had to do something to repay the favour. The one thing The Playhouse and The Apollo had in common was having a chippy nearby. It was the least I could do. I had never been in an Edinburgh chippy before.

I may already have mentioned that true Glaswegians already know how this story ends. Suffice to say, in the moments after the wrapping of the fish suppers, and before payment was made, I heard words that sent shockwaves through my very core.

I was still reeling when we got back to the car and could barely enjoy my feast because of what I had just heard.

As we rolled back along the M8, past Harthill Services, we felt the need to roll the windows down a little bit. The windows were steaming up but the main reason was the smell of fish, and chips, and batter, and salt and *sauce*!

IT'S NO FUN GETTIN'
HIT ON THE HEAD WITH A
F****N, BEER CAN

Six cans of Kestral and a window seat all to ourselves on the train. JJB and me were set fair for our first trip to a festival. I don't know what the optimal time is for two 18-year-olds to drink six cans of Kestral but, considering the journey time from Glasgow Central to Balloch is an hour at most that equates to just under 20 minutes per can. Seems reasonable.

The Loch Lomond Rock Festival was the magnet drawing us. We went on the Saturday. The Sunday was a bit on the heavy rock side, although Lindisfarne might dispute that. But the Saturday was all about new, raw, current, vibrant, challenging talent.

We had mixed feelings about Balloch and Loch Lomond. On the one hand, it seemed like such a perfect idea: close enough to Glasgow that the journey time didn't present a problem, but far enough away that it felt like a bit of a day out. On the other, Billy Connolly had ripped the you know what out of the Aran-knit hikers and folk singers and Balloch was one of the places he identified as *their* territory. Hilarious, yes, but there was that connotation, that connection. The weather was drab, and wet. Cagoules were essential. We didn't want anyone to think we were going to burst into *The Wanderlust Song* at the drop of a bobble hat.

We overcompensated by loudly discussing the acts we were most keen to see. Stiff Little Fingers featured heavily. So did The Tourists and The Jam. The only song we knew by The Regents was *7Teen*, but they would be worth seeing anyway. We probably wouldn't get there in time for The Chords.

JJB already had 'Inflammable Material'. He had decided to become a punk, but a sort of part-time, aspirational, half-arsed punk. He was happy to colour his hair, but only with blue food dye which would wash out. He sometimes wore a white boiler suit with names of bands and rude slogans written all over it. He would pogo, but he wouldn't spit. There were no piercings. A career in insurance beckoned.

As we sat on the train, none of the above was in evidence. We disposed of our empties in the bins provided, picked up our Cagoules and headed off to wherever it was that this festival was taking place.

***

Three things struck me the minute we arrived. The first was inevitable: mud. But it doesn't matter how inevitable mud is, it is still mud and there is no pleasure to be found in wading through it. The second was the tension. There was a febrile atmosphere. It was coming from one tribe on one side and another tribe on the other. Punks versus mods. This wasn't looking good. The third thing that struck me was just how big it was. Not the site, not The Bear Park, not the stage, but the tongue. Buster Bloodvessel's tongue.

We did indeed miss The Chords so Bad Manners were on stage when we arrived. The set was predictable. Bad Manners were riding high in the charts and riding their luck as a novelty act-cum-ska band making some bucks when the going was good. When they appeared on TV, their USP was the lead singer, Buster Bloodvessel. His size was one thing, his energy another. But his tongue was his trademark. Viewers were amazed and sickened in equal measure as his tongue protruded, waggled this way and that and took on a life of its own as Buster sang *Lip Up Fatty* and *Ne-Ne Na-Na Na-Na Nu-Nu*. A great asset for TV but would it work on stage?

It didn't seem to matter how far from the stage we were, his tongue was clearly visible. When we arrived and made our way forward it was the one feature that jumped out from the leaden backdrop. It wasn't mobbed, it was still early in the day, so we could move closer to the front with ease, but something was holding us back. We told ourselves it was because of the simmering, impending, battle between the punks and mods. But maybe we were just scared of being bound up on the insides of this slavering giant bounding up and down before us.

***

The Cuban Heels, a band which grew out of the first incarnation of Simple Minds, were on next but we were already getting excited about Stiff Little Fingers. We sought out food and dipped in and out of the other acts, making sure we caught *7Teen* by The Regents. Sometimes it rained, sometimes the rain stopped. The only constant was the aggression, the feeling that something nasty was in the air.

***

Finally, the moment arrived. Stiff Little Fingers were about to take to the stage and their arrival became the first trigger point for the combatants. Of all the bands who performed that day Stiff Little Fingers were the epitome of punk. Their songs were short, loud, angry and full of venom. Their targets were clear. They railed against the Troubles. They railed against racism. They railed against pretty much everything. But they did, actually, have something to say. This wasn't shock for the sake of shock, or comedy. This wasn't *Kill* by Alberto Y Lost Trios Paranoias. This wasn't Jilted John. Sitting down with a copy of 'Inflammable Material' on a turntable is not a relaxing experience but is one worth experiencing just the same. If you can get the words in front of you, and try to make them out over the cacophony of noise, you will have an insight into the backdrop of the 70s as they moved into the 80s.

Thankfully, the rain had stopped but a different kind of rain descended from the sky. Missiles. Skirmishes were breaking out near the front. The bouncers moved in.

'Hey! Leave him alone. There's only one of him and loads of you.'

Jake Burns had spoken. It was an interesting tactic. It could easily have sparked a riot but he had a confidence and an assuredness about him. Punks, mods and bouncers all seemed to take note. Order, of a kind, was restored and Stiff Little Fingers filled the early evening air with the green of their homeland and the blue of their language. The red mist of anger had subsided, for now.

The peace was never going to hold. Stiff Little Fingers ripped through their repertoire. JJB and I gazed in awe at this force of nature, all the time noting the surrounding temperature and wondering when it would all kick off again. And kick off it did. Halfway through a three-minute rant about some injustice or other, the cans flew again. Stiff Little Fingers continued as if nothing had happened. The song finished, seemingly as quickly as it had started, and Jake Burns spoke.

'Right, that's enough. It's no fun gettin' hit on the head with a f****n' beer can.'

And peace descended on The Bonnie Banks once more.

***

JJB was more into The Tourists than I was but The Jam were top of the bill. We could hardly come here and not see The Jam. But there was a feeling of emptiness now that Stiff Little Fingers had finished. There was a feeling that they just couldn't be topped. At least Jake Burns had brought some order to proceedings.

We started to consider our options. What time were The Jam due on stage? What time was the last train? I remembered Billy Connolly's song *Last Train Tae Glasgow Central*. Then I thought about those girls from Aberdeen who came to Glasgow to see The Bay City Rollers and missed the last train and had to spend the night hanging around the station. We were in the middle of nowhere. What if *we* missed the last train home?

The Tourists had started their set. JJB was enjoying it but was still talking about Stiff Little Fingers. He kept saying, 'It's no fun gettin' hit on the head with a f****n' beer can', in his best Belfast accent. The conversation turned to The Jam, and the time of the last train, and the bubbling red volcanic lava that was mingling with the greenish, yellowy bile that spewed in equal measure from the punks and mods. The Tourists sang *So Good To Be Back Home Again*.

We made an executive decision. Head for the train. We missed The Jam.

It seems like an act of treason to have had such an opportunity and to walk away from it, but festival organisers and train companies didn't seem to coordinate things back then. If we had stayed to watch The Jam, we would have missed the *Last Train Tae Glasgow Central*. We would have had to spend the night in a bear park for God's sake. But something tells me that the bears wouldn't have been the most frightening creatures that night.

'AH'M GOIN' A KILLIN'

The Sands Family are a talented bunch. Tommy has already had a brief mention and yes, I saw him sing *There Were Roses*, a poignant take on the mindless logic of the Troubles. That was at Glasgow's St Andrews in the Square. Serious stuff indeed. But he also sang *Humpty Dumpty Was Pushed*, so there was stuff in there to make you smile as well. He talked about the work he had done with prisoners in US jails and how he tried to engage them through music. He talked of trying to find something that he had in common with them and that they had in common with each other. It proved difficult. But he focused on one of the most basic tunes in music, *Twinkle Twinkle Little Star*. There is barely a child in the world that has never heard it and so, through the simplest of tunes, he gradually built up a rapport, found a common interest and helped in some small way to make a breakthrough, and a difference.

Tommy's brother, Colum, is also worth spending a few minutes on. There was one particular festival at which I saw him perform. There were some similarities to Tommy in that he had light and shade, some damned serious material and some light, knockabout, make-the-audience-laugh-out-loud stuff. But the two were not the same. Sure, they may have achieved the same appreciation, adulation and respect from their audiences, but their styles were different. Colum seemed to have a bit of bounce in the way he moved, the way he spoke and the stories he told. He told us of some obstacles he had had to overcome to be with us that evening.

Colum had found himself in Ireland, as opposed to Northern Ireland. To get to Scotland, he would need to cross the border to get the ferry and then travel across country to be with us. During the first leg of his journey he would have to pass the border checkpoints. When he got there he was asked where he was going.

'Ah'm goin' a Killin', he replied.

Somehow, he managed to get through and wound his way across the sea and across the country, slowing down as he neared his destination to take in the beauty of the Falls of Dochart and then down the hill to The McLaren Hall. Colum was indeed goin' a Killin, he was on the bill at the Killin Festival.

***

Killin is a beautiful place. Small, but beautiful. Someone had the idea to put on a traditional music festival in the village so the entire traditional music fraternity flocked there for one weekend in June and the village pulsated in a way that it seldom had before. The weather was usually rubbish. I can only recall two sunny days in eight years. They should have had it in Glasgow in May, but then it wouldn't have been what it was.

Lonesome Dave made the arrangements the first time we went. We chose the hotel right beside the Falls of Dochart. Two couples, two rooms, one en suite, one not. That wasn't contentious at all! It didn't matter too much as we didn't spend much time in our rooms. If we got off the mark quickly enough on the Friday we could stop in Callendar for pizza and get to Killin in time for the night's entertainment. Saturday afternoon was picnic time. That didn't always go too well. That first year we drank wine and ate crusty bread, cheese and pate on a barbeque bench in the hotel's beer garden. We had to wrap up warm. That was one of the more successful Saturdays. In the second year the Saturday was a scorcher. We had decamped to the Killin Hotel on the grounds that they had more en suite rooms and it was just across the road from The McLaren Hall. The hotel, and its grounds, heaved and buzzed. We found a spot on the grass by the river and barbecued chicken. I sat, drinking this in, listening to someone picking on a banjo. The sound travelled on the air. Sometimes it was interrupted with the hubbub of noise that came from the stalls where venison burgers could be had. Then it would calm down and the banjo would return, and all was right with the world.

The banjo player turned out to be Billy Connolly. He emerged from the riverbank just as I was making my way down there for some, unimportant, unremembered reason. I recognised him instantly. For a fleeting moment I wondered if he remembered borrowing a pen from me in 1975. I felt the need to say something.

'This is beautiful, isn't it?'

'Yes.'

That was all he said, but he said it in that very Billy Connolly way. It was definite, it was emphatic, there was an elongated 's' sound at the end.

'Yesssssss.'

He went on his way. He clearly wanted to be incognito. Some hope.

***

The queue for The McLaren Hall started to form early. Everyone had been to the hotels, cafes and pubs for an early dinner and now it was time to grab a seat as close to the front as possible. Billy Connolly had chosen a different strategy. He waited until the eateries were emptying and then went out with his two daughters. I figured he was probably used to people finding him a good seat in most places he went. It wouldn't be any different here. As we queued, The Big Yin was making his way back to the Killin Hotel, daughters at his side, his arms round their shoulders.

The queue ranged from the sober to the tipsy to the downright drunk and, as we know, drunk people are braver than sober people. Some of the drunk people started goading Connolly. The drunks were far enough away that they didn't fear any recriminations. They had got away with it the night before, even prompted a bit of a reaction. To them, Connolly was fair game, and with those two daughters beside him there was only so much he could do.

Most people would have seen a father with his two girls, sauntering down a quiet village street in the evening sunshine. The drunks saw a chance to grab some limelight for themselves.

'Haw, Big Yin.'

'It's amazin' the surge of strength ye get when ye bite yer ain willy!'

Most people in the queue rolled their eyes and tut-tutted.

'Wallop. Jaggy bunnet right on the heid!'

They were doing Billy Connolly's greatest hits, but there was no sense of fun, no acknowledgement of the joy these routines had brought. There was a sneering tone. They thought he was there for the taking.

The family of three continued to saunter. As they reached the hotel they had to turn so that their backs were to the queue. The bating continued.

'If it wisny fur yer wellies, where would ye be?'

Billy Connolly may have been about 500yds away but he silenced the drunks in one movement. He took his hand off one of the girl's shoulders, lifted it into the air and raised his middle finger. He replaced his hand where it had been. Perfect comedy timing. His two girls had no idea what he had done but the queue laughed and the drunks were silenced and, even when Connolly was ushered into his seat in the balcony just after the show began, the drunks said no more.

'Cop yer whack for that!'

***

To have a star of such magnitude as Billy Connolly, even as a spectator, was rare for Killin. It wasn't about superstars. It was about the love of music and the love of tradition. I will elaborate on that shortly, but first I want to dwell briefly on a famous Scottish trait.

Having acknowledged that Scotland lost the Hampden international to England in 1982 it seems only fair that we should discuss the Rugby World Cup semi-final of 1995. I found myself in the bar of the Killin Hotel, craning my neck to see the small TV in the corner. England versus the All Blacks was a tasty prospect. With the match coming at such a crucial stage of the competition, the anticipation and excitement was a high as it could be.

One of the reasons we were squeezed in near the bar was that a bunch of musicians had laid out some chairs, in a circle, in the middle of the floor and were collaboratin', improvisin' and jammin'. Dougie MacLean was among them. The musicians didn't appear to have any interest in the rugby. They sat, in the round, lank hair drooping over their shoulders, the grey pallor of fags and sleep deprivation clouding all of their faces. As they downed one pint, more would appear, a constant stream of dark ales with foamy heads as feet tapped, guitars twanged and fiddles fiddled.

Back at the bar, heads bobbed from side to side as the whistle blew and the semi-final was up and running. As the ensemble in the circle played, fingers thrummed against legs and drummed on the counter. Feet tapped and heads craned to see the start of the action. Tenners were waved in the air in the hope that the holder would be noticed as the bar staff tried to keep up with the rush, the demand, the thirst. And while one part of the room pulsated in time to the action, another held a steady rhythm with one musician giving way to another, oblivious to the jostling and jockeying and the sporting history that was about to unfold.

It only took four minutes for the first roar to shake the room. Jona Lomu trampled his way through England's defence and within minutes the All Blacks had scored again. Smiles appeared on faces, backs were slapped, high fives went all around and there wasn't a Kiwi in sight.

Still, the steady beat was held. Sometimes a reel, sometimes a jig, occasionally a slow air. The custodians of the traditional music scene had more important things to do than watch rugby.

New Zealand were toying with England now. A penalty, then a drop goal, then another try. The game was over as a contest by half-time. But that wasn't the point. The Scots in the All Black's tops were testament to that. The teams came out for the second half and Lomu went over again. The cheers and the yells from the rugby watchers threatened to drown out the session. The circular supergroup was having none of it. They must have picked up on the atmosphere. One minute they were lost in a world of their own, the next they were starting a party. As the scoreboard ticked ever higher in New Zealand's favour the pace of the session increased. They were now playing with the intensity normally reserved for the later part of a gig when the audience is in the palm of the musician's hands and ready to let themselves go.

No one knew any New Zealand traditions, other than the sacrosanct Haka, and no one was messing with that, so the 'hoochs' and 'choochs' would need to do. The heads gradually turned away from the screen and into the middle of the room. People sang and danced and laughed. They glanced at the TV screen to see how the match would finish, but it didn't matter so much now. There wouldn't be a tense ending, just a drubbing. Time for a party and we had the best house band you could ever wish for.

***

Better people than me have psycho-analysed the minds of us Scots, particularly in a sporting context. Starved of our own success, we look elsewhere for sporting glory. Often it takes the form of supporting whoever is playing against England. It's a kind of back-handed compliment to the Auld Enemy. England did go on to win the Rugby World Cup eight years later. They had also won the football World Cup in 1966. For English people these successes seem few and far between. Most other nations would trade their gross domestic product to put those two triumphs in their empty trophy cabinets.

***

The atmosphere in the Killin Hotel that day wasn't toxic. It was good natured. Painful for the few brave souls in the white shirts, but not vitriolic, and they took it in good part.

I still think back on it. Sometimes it makes me smile. Sometimes I question myself and those around me.

I answered the phone one Monday afternoon in 2015. It was the day after Scotland were robbed of a place in the Rugby World Cup semi-final by a bad refereeing decision. On the other end of the line was a friend – a rugby-mad friend; a rugby-mad English friend. He was gutted. He had spent the Sunday afternoon transfixed by events at Twickenham as Scotland battled, against the odds, to overcome Australia. Scotland were given no chance but came close just the same. My friend had been cheering Scotland on. He felt bad for me, and for the whole of Scotland, and for Scots the world over. It wasn't an anti-Australia thing. He just wanted Scotland to win. I felt suitably chastened.

Had Scotland won it would have been a semi-final against Argentina. Winnable. And then a final against, guess who, New Zealand. Australia turned out to be the All Blacks' opponents in that final and the All Blacks trounced them. It would have been a different story if the All Blacks had played Scotland. Once their Haka was over, we would have set up a session on the centre spot and, as our musicians provided the inspiration, we would have danced rings around the All Blacks, and the rest, as they say, would have been history.

***

You would struggle to find a top-40 artist at Killin. It wasn't that kind of festival. What you would find would be accomplished singers, musicians, performers and dancers. You would find artists who could make themselves cry while trying to sing a self-composition about a parent.

You would find artists who could make the audience howl with laughter and those who would expose the modern-day, West End composers for pillaging traditional tunes and passing them off as their own. But most of all, you would find versatility.

Karine Polwart was given the briefest of mentions earlier and deserves more than that because, on the night she was due to play Killin, it was to be as part of MacAlias. This was, essentially, Karine Polwart and Gill Bowman in what turned out to be an all-too-short collaboration. When MacAlias took to the stage, there was something missing – Gill Bowman.

Karine addressed the audience. They had prepared, they had rehearsed, Gill had travelled but she was ill. Karine was on her own. We listened patiently. We weren't sure what this meant. Karine managed our expectations. She would do her best. She would sing a few songs, some that MacAlias would have sung, some of her own. Wow! If she busked that gig, it was easy to see why she would rise to the top and win the awards. Versatility – that's what comes from years of hard graft, a passion for music and, of course, talent.

***

But the last word on Killin should go to the unsung heroes, not those who receive the adulation on the main stage but the artists who exhibited their wares at the craft fare. The rocking-horse maker who seemed to have all day to talk about his creations, even if he never got an order. The storytelling session in the pub, away on the outskirts of the village.

The moothie workshop will live long in the memory. It started at about 10.30am in Fishers Hotel. That time in the morning is early for a festival crowd but for some it was just an extension of the previous night. The moothie expert showed us a selection of moothies. He blew into them and discussed the range of sounds that came from each one. It was like looking at a miniaturised version of electric guitars, all lined up across a stage. He played some tunes but somehow the session didn't flow.

'Play the blues' came a shout.

The moothie man smiled politely and carried on, but there is no stopping someone who has gone beyond the pale.

'Play the blues' came another gibbering interruption.

The moothie man persevered. Well-intentioned attendees asked questions. How long had he been playing the moothie? How did he learn? When did he learn? Did he ever play the moothie in a band?

'Come on man, show us how to play the blues.'

And on and on it went.

The moothie man was unruffled. He had a job to do and he carried on and did it. I'm sure, if he had wanted to, he could have played the blues. But he didn't. So there.

***

When we saw the poster for Appalachian clog dancing we had to see what it was all about. The group, mostly female, clicked and tapped their clogs in perfect harmony on the wooden floor of The McLaren Hall. This would never be the headline act, but the synchronicity of it was mesmerising. And the noise. It reverberated all around and the tunes embedded themselves in our heads as we returned to the village, pretending we could do it just as well as the experts. If we had to perfect our technique a bit we could deal with that at the workshop the next morning.

The turnout was astonishing. A huge circle was formed with the cloggers in the middle showing us how it was done. They ran through a few trial runs and then it was time for us to have a go. The tunes from the day before struck up again and we moved, clockwise, in our circle, trying to get somewhere close to what we had been shown. The atmosphere was fabulous. Even if one student clogger crashed into another it was all part of the fun. On we went, clogging our hearts out, with proper cloggers intervening from time to time to put us right on our technique and keep the whole thing flowing along beautifully.

There were chairs around the hall. In a break from the dancing I scanned the room. Everyone was buzzing, waiting for the next tune. As the cloggers gave out more instructions I noticed that every seat was empty except for one, which was occupied by a puffing and panting Lonesome Dave. He had had enough. He would never make it as a clogger, not like me.

We clogged on for a while longer, the real cloggers correcting our faults, demonstrating how it should be done. There was one clogger in particular. She was young and beautiful. How had she got into clogging? She looked as if she had the world at her feet. She was so nice, so friendly, so engaging. When she came over to help the world seemed like a sunnier place.

Lonesome Dave was a spent force. There would be no second wind for him. I clogged on, hoping that my next instruction would come from her.

The pace of the music intensified and the clogging became more arduous, but it was infectious and addictive too. People whooped and cheered and feet thumped on the floor; the click-clack of the real cloggers kept us in time. I glanced into the centre. It had been a while since anyone had given me an instruction. I assumed I had cracked it but then saw her coming towards me.

I clogged like I had never clogged before. She had told me earlier that I was inclined to move upwards when I needed a downward motion to get the desired effect. I tried with every fibre of my being to obey. Now it was my turn for an appraisal again. I was hoping for a good report.

'Tell me, have you ever done any morris dancing?'

I have never lived it down. I have never tried morris dancing either but it doesn't seem to stop me being a natural. If I ever find a maypole I will gladly dance around it, but only on condition that I don't need to wave any ribbons or wear a silly hat and that I get to wear shoes that click and clack.

CREDIT WHERE CREDIT'S DUE

TIME TO FLY

None of the above would have happened without people. A few names have cropped up time and again. The Shugmeister, JJB, Lonesome Dave. But there is one person who hasn't had a mention and who deserves the biggest mention of all. Someone who was beside me through many of the stories you have just read and made a suggestion here and a suggestion there. Someone who was willing to try something new, to go in a different direction, to keep an open mind.

We came across The John Wright Band from time to time. John Wright worked as a shepherd in the borders. That's what he told us. I had no reason to disbelieve him. He painted beautiful, verbal pictures of clear night skies in which stars shone down on a tranquil, silent part of the planet. He was also a beautiful singer. His band's repertoire was wide and varied and they always told stories of how the songs evolved, what they meant and the writers behind them. Credit where credit's due.

There was one song in particular that jumped out, *What's the Use of Wings*? The song was written by Brian Bedford and champions some of the unheralded things in life. The bonsai tree, the pony, the myna bird, the angelfish, the snowy owl. It goes further than that, though. It explores how each was shackled and prevented from growing, exploring, speaking, stretching out and flying. The saddest thing is that they were left to believe that this had been done for their own good. The bonsai tree had its roots bound, the myna bird was caged and told what to say. The pony was made to work and the angelfish taken from vast waters and placed in a world so small it had nowhere to go.

What about the snowy owl? Imagine what it must be like to have wings, to soar above the earth and to swoop and gather what you need. Imagine if *we* had wings. What would we swoop and gather? We could follow the sun; we could have free entry to as many festivals as we liked and we could live in a world free of the Boundary Charge. Enough people have written songs about wings to show their symbolic importance. Perhaps you have felt the need to spread yours, or maybe you need some wind beneath them, or, if you're lucky, you could be flying high upon the wings of love. But if you're not so lucky you might have broken wings. Could you learn to fly again? That depends.

The snowy owl's wings weren't broken, they had been clipped. In many ways that's worse. Someone, for their own convenience, chose to do this to a great bird whose instinct was to explore vast, cavernous, open spaces, unrestricted. Some birds can regrow their feathers. Regaining their confidence and trust is another matter. Our friend the snowy owl did not.

Our wings are metaphoric but they exist just the same. Listen to *The Cape* by Kathy Mattea. On one level it's a light-hearted song about someone who believes they can fly and keeps falling flat on their face. But, as Douglas Adams told us, flying is just a matter of aiming for the ground and making sure you miss. That's what our friend with the cape did and guess what. One day he flew.

I once found that my own wings were struggling to support me. Would they heal or were they irreparably broken? Things weren't going so well and it seemed as if the world was closing in. I was in a cage, or was it a tank? I was dancing to other peoples' tunes, trying to please everyone, and failing. And then I remembered that song.

'What's the use of wings if you can't fly?'

There are so many sad sentiments in that song but for me, it's about being given the freedom to express yourself, the trust that you will know what to do with that freedom, and the hope that the trust will be repaid. I'm glad I remembered that song. It helped a lot but it would be more accurate to say that a certain someone reminded me that it existed.

With Love and Thanks xxxxx.

TIME TO GO

To conclude, nothing you have read matters much in the grand scheme of things, except that last bit and maybe the polite vagrants, even the one I saw finish his shift, hand over to his mate and hail a taxi! How dare he? I watched this as I sat in Di Maggios, eating pizza, drinking beer, all warm and cosy. There are some contradictions in there but trying to find solutions rather than the contradictions would be more helpful.

As for the gigs, a list of dates, times, support acts and set lists would have been interesting and informative. Thank goodness there are people in the world who make these available. But this book was never intended as a reference point for fact-crazed anoraks. If you decided to read this and that was your expectation, I apologise for wasting your time. However, I hope, even if you felt cheated to begin with, that you got something out of it. If you are still reading, maybe you did.

I have tried to be as accurate as possible at every stage, but what you have read are memories. If you can say with absolute certainty that Al Green handed out carnations rather than roses, or if you can name the offending member of Capercaillie on the night of the 1999 Champions League Final, or if you have cast-iron evidence that Slade did play Chipping Norton, Shepton Mallet and Mönchengladbach, I doff my cap to you.

If you are left with any unanswered questions, I admire you for your forbearance. Most people will have moved on with their lives by now. However, just in case it matters to anyone, Lonesome Dave and The Blues Cowboys are a figment of an imagination. Not mine, but Lonesome Dave's. Any similarities to real Lonesome Daves or real Blues Cowboys are entirely unintentional.

Here's one last thing. You may remember that I mercilessly mocked the Sydney branch of The Humpff Family for filming road signs to show to the folks back home. Yes, it's bizarre, but maybe that's all I've done here. Maybe I've just erected some signposts or stuck some flags on a map. If so, I hope you enjoyed the journey.

In the end, when all is said and done, a man went to some gigs and had a good time. I know, it's only rock 'n' roll... but I'm quite partial to it.

More from K. A. Arnside ...

You can keep up with K. A. Arnside's news and events and register for updates at: kaarnside.com

K. A. Arnside is also on Facebook and Twitter.

CPSIA information can be obtained
at www.ICGtesting.com
Printed in the USA
BVHW081312010622
638618BV00006B/74